Shahram Khosravi (ed.)
Waiting – A Project in Conversation

Culture & Theory | Volume 243

Shahram Khosravi is a professor of social anthropology at Stockholm University. His research interests include anthropology of Iran and the Middle East, migration, forced displacement, and border studies.

Shahram Khosravi (ed.)
Waiting – A Project in Conversation

[transcript]

Bibliographic information published by the Deutsche Nationalbibliothek
The Deutsche Nationalbibliothek lists this publication in the Deutsche Nationalbibliografie; detailed bibliographic data are available in the Internet at http://dnb.d-nb.de

© 2021 transcript Verlag, Bielefeld

All rights reserved. No part of this book may be reprinted or reproduced or utilized in any form or by any electronic, mechanical, or other means, now known or hereafter invented, including photocopying and recording, or in any information storage or retrieval system, without permission in writing from the publisher.

Cover layout: Maria Arndt, Bielefeld
Cover illustration: Shahram Khosravi
Layout: Matthew Ashton
Printed by Majuskel Medienproduktion GmbH, Wetzlar
Print-ISBN 978-3-8376-5458-5
PDF-ISBN 978-3-8394-5458-9
https://doi.org/10.14361/9783839454589

Printed on permanent acid-free text paper.

Contents

Preface 9

Prelude I. The Weight of Waiting 13

    Waiting
    Faith Wilding 27
    Care to Wait
    Jenny Richards and Gunilla Lundahl 33
    The Sea is Mohammad al-Khatib's
    Adania Shibli 51
    Sandhours
    Majd Abdel Hamid 57

Prelude II. Stolen Time 65

    Undocumented: The Architecture of Migrant Detention
    Tings Chak 71
    Remain
    Hoda Afshar 81
    Arriving to Depart
    Omid Tofighian 89
    Refugees Welcome?
    Hayfaa Chalabi 97
    Asymmetries
    Alessandro Petti, Sandi Hilal, and Salvatore Porcaro 105

Prelude III. Waiting among Dead Trees 113

Ecologies of Waiting: Stories of a Vacant Land
Sepideh Karami.. 117
after the blast: near silence, rising
mirko nikolić 129

Prelude IV. Standing in Line 137

Queues
Golrokh Nafisi.. 141
The Distance from Here
Bani Abidi.. 143
Waiting in Queues under Dictatorship
Basma Abdel Aziz... 151
Our Silence will Swell Like a Mountain
Omar Berrada...157
A Tenuous Case of Trust
Omid Mehrgan... 171

Contributors... 181

Preface

Shahram Khosravi

The idea for this book came about from a failure, as I began to realise that the research project on waiting which I had been working on did not make sense when presented in a purely academic form. I failed to discuss the concept or practices of waiting in a format suitable for peer-reviewed journals, higher seminars and conference papers. Over the last decade I have conducted different, yet somehow interconnected fieldwork which directly or indirectly relates to waiting, time, and temporalities; from vulnerable young people in Iran, to following irregular migrants stuck in various camps in Greece, to deportees to Afghanistan. I've seen many people in prolonged situations of waiting and have listened to countless stories about their lived experiences of temporal stuckedness, however, every time I attempted to transform these experiences and stories into academic texts I felt like a failure. Why?

I have no answers, only vague guesses. Waiting is about the senses. If you do not sense it, there is no waiting. We sense waiting in the form of boredom, despair, anxiety and restlessness, but also anticipation and hope. Prolonged waiting is like insomnia—a state of wakefulness, a kind of mood, an emotional state. But it is also about politics; affecting and affected by gender, citizenship, class and race. It surfaces in the gaps between trust and betrayed promises, between expectations and coloniality.

I decided to approach waiting with the help of visual artists, poets, architects, fiction writers, photographers and curators who have worked on the theme. They generously accepted my invitation and joined me in a conversation on waiting. Their works in this book cover different forms of waiting, over diverse geographies, and with attention to key aspects such as gender, class, and race.

I am deeply indebted to them for sharing their work in this book. I am also grateful to Jacek Smolicki, Jacqueline Hoàng Nguyễn, Maryam Omrani, Paolo Favero, Behzad Khosravi Noori, Erling Björgvinsson, Sarah Philipson Isaac, Annika Lindberg and Mahmoud Keshavarz for their intellectual engagement in this project. Many thanks to Christine Jacobsen at the University of Bergen and other members of the research project WAIT for a long and inspiring conversation on waiting. I also thank Dagmawi Yimer for the pleasure I had in our collaboration for making the video *Waiting* in the Summer of 2019. I thank Matthew Ashton for his contribution to the book's graphic design and layout. Thank you to the Research Council of Norway and the Swedish Council for Working Life and Social Research for financial support.

Finally the ones who are thanked without any particular reason are Nina, Kian, and Mimi.

The result is in your hands. I hope you enjoy the book as much as I did.

The Weight of Waiting

Shahram Khosravi

This book took its final form during the COVID-19 pandemic when the whole world was waiting, and as I write these words in July 2020, it still seems suspended in uncertainty. During the current global lockdown, nobody knows what is awaiting us and, even worse, what exactly we are waiting for; the world is bored.

People from East to West are waiting for a return to their 'normal' life. We all wait, but we wait differently. While the wealthy wait in self-isolation on private islands, others cannot afford quarantine. The poor cannot afford to wait. Reports coming from different corners of the world testify that the poor and marginalised are dying at disproportionate rates compared with more privileged members of society. While the pandemic affects everyone, disregarding race and class, the consequences of the outbreak are diverse, just like waiting. We all wait, but the experience of waiting is different for different people. Prolonged waiting not only engenders new vulnerabilities, but also aggravates vulnerabilities that are already present, revealing socio-political regulations that result in an unequal distribution of risk and hope. Waiting is not a neutral condition, but rather a hierarchical interwoven complex of gender, race, and class. Waiting, thus, is pre-eminently a political issue.

One of the basic divisions in the world today is between those who are forced into protracted conditions of waiting and those who impose it. Waiting is a particular experience of time, and has become a powerful technique for the regulation of social interactions between individuals, as well as between individuals and the authorities.

Waiting is a dialectical relationship in which the logic of *waiting for* and *to be waited for* meet—a matter of power relations through the manipulation of others' time. When in contact with bureaucracy, individuals wait for their turn and for the officials' decisions. Being kept in a state of protracted waiting is used as a dramaturgical means of mystification and an expression of power[1]—to keep people waiting, without ruining their hope, is an exercise of power over other people's time[2] in order to preserve dependency and subordination. The neoliberal technologies of citizenship enacted through keeping people waiting for jobs, education, housing, health care, social welfare, or pensions turn citizens into 'patients of the state.'[3]

Protracted waiting and mystification make life unpredictable and engenders uncertainties, generating the feeling that one is not fully in command of one's life. Marginalised groups find themselves in a race against time, with a sense of being 'left behind' of what is assumed to be the natural rhythm of modern life, lacking the power to go forward.

When social life is suspended one feels a lack of integration into 'national time.' Suffering from perpetual suspension and the predicament of being 'stuck,' in a prolonged wait for a job, a house, an education, marriage, a visa, or asylum, makes people feel out of sync with others and surrounded by a growing sense of disconnectedness. Time is often associated with success and money and waiting therefore symbolises waste, emptiness and uselessness—there is a discrepancy

---

1 Erving Goffman, *The Presentation of Self in Everyday Life* (New York: Doubleday and Company, 1959).

2 Pierre Bourdieu, *Pascalian Meditations* (Stanford: University Press, 2000).

3 Javier Auyero, *Patients of the State: The Politics of Waiting in Argentina* (Durham: Duke University Press, 2012).

between common social goals (speed, mobility, the idea that time is money) and the reality of individuals' socio-political capacities, with more and more people feeling unable to move forward in life at the speed expected of larger society.

This systemic mismatch has made waiting a central element to the relationship between everyday life and capitalism. The last century was one of promising images and dreams of welfare, a stable life cycle, *law and order*, distribution of human rights, and in some parts of the world, equal distribution of wealth and social justice. While we have witnessed these promises slowly fade away, we no longer know anymore exactly what we are waiting for—this is what makes capitalism boring. Walter Benjamin writes in the Arcades Project that "we are bored when we do not know what we are waiting for" and then asks, "what is the dialectical antithesis to boredom?"[4] His answer is awakening into a historical wakefulness.

A few years ago, Neda, a young Iranian woman, told me that the whole of her childhood was spent waiting for asylum in Germany. When she was in her late teens, one day her mother rushed into her room screaming with joy and showed her a letter saying their application had finally been approved. Then Neda started crying and asked: "did we suffer so much and for so long just for a piece of paper?"

The moment Neda felt she had lost her childhood waiting for "a piece of paper" was the moment she experienced time in its historical and political sense. The moment of realising that one's time is killed and stolen is the moment that waiting time is demystified and is unpacked from its ideological layers. It is the moment waiting time appears denaturalised and therefore also historicised.[5] It is when Neda became aware of the meaningless purpose of her waiting, since "the piece of paper" did not change anything about their socio-economic

---

4 Walter Benjamin, The Arcades Project (Cambridge, MA: Belknap Press, 1999), 105.
5 Omid Mehrgan, "Az Zaman-e Baghimandeh," *Herfeh Honarmand*, No 41. (Spring 1391/2012): 163–171.

condition, but rather commenced a new waiting; "to be integrated into German society." Shocked by a sudden uncertainty about *what* exactly she had been waiting for and accordingly *why*, Neda was overwhelmed by a profound ennui. Neda's ennui should not be reduced to bafflement, an emotional reaction to the long and painful wait for only "a piece of paper," but rather it should be seen as a significant political interrogation. Experiencing ennui and being bored, in Benjaminian meaning, is productive, engendering consciousness about the social and political condition of waiting. Awaking from a purposeless waiting is a transformation. For Benjamin, the revolutionary energies of boredom are exactly this; "boredom is the threshold to great deeds."[6] While crossing the threshold one "takes in the time and renders it up in altered form—that of expectation."[7] Expectation is a transformation of time, pregnant with potentialities and possibilities for a counter-mood to boredom.

When the illusion that we know what we are waiting for is replaced by an awareness of the emptiness and boredom of waiting, new subjectivities emerge and there is a chance for revolutionary pessimism.

The revolutionary unwaiting

Historical wakefulness out of an awaiting without an object emerges from pain. The word patience comes from the Latin word pati, which means 'to suffer.' As Dostoevsky famously put it—"suffering is the sole origin of consciousness."[8] Suffering may indeed lead to perplexity over all hardships during waiting; but it may also raise significant political questions and demands for understanding *what* waiting has been about.

---

6 Benjamin, *The Arcades Project*, 105.

7 Ibid., 107.

8 Fyodor Dostoyevsky, *Notes from the Underground* (1861; repr., London: Alma Classics, 2014), 32.

Hence, it is no accident that etymologically, the word *wait* is derived from the words *to watch* and to *be awake*. Waiting engenders wakefulness and vigilance. Waiting is being in a state of consciousness. The person in a state of waiting constantly thinks about her or his waiting. Waiting means constantly updating oneself about the social and political condition waiting has imposed on her or him. Wakefulness makes waiting similar to insomnia, that is, a compulsion to be *vigilant* and pay attention to what is happing around oneself. Similar to the one who waits, the insomniac thinks about the reasons for her insomnia and seeks relief from it. This aspect of waiting is even more palpable in the French verb *attendre*, which means *to direct one's mind toward*. A waiting-towards the not-yet is attentive and oriented.

What keeps the person awake in prolonged waiting is not measuring chronological time, *Chronos*; but chasing moments of potential opening, *Kairos*. Approaching waiting as a state of wakeful navigation and vigilance here refers to the qualities of time, what Greeks called *Kairos*, i.e. critical moments when things can happen and openings for changes may ensue. Lack of mobility in time and space associated with waiting (usually expressed as *going nowhere in life*), does not mean lack of mobilisation. Navigation through the spatio-temporal contexts of waiting might create openings for new political orientations. An interesting example are protests by migrants and refugees—from Moria camp on the Greek island of Lesbos and Calais in the north France, to the striking mobilisations of the inmates in Australia's notorious detention centre on Manus Island, and sit-in protests in major European cities—triggering a subjectivity through the actions of politics. For these people, waiting has become a state of wakefulness engaged with potentialities for a different future.

The future is not a section of a linear timeline, which will come after the present, but is rather in a constant dialectical relationship with the present. All struggles, strategies and tactics, navigations and wakefulness of waiting are animated through the constant interplay between the now and the not-yet. Waiting (the now) is not suspended time oriented through a temporal progression towards a future (end of waiting); but rather, the now and the not-yet constantly make and remake each other. Dialectical wakefulness between the now and the not-yet generates hopeful visions and practices. Even in the form of daydreaming, these practices are agentive. Daydreaming, orienting oneself toward not-yet fulfilled promises, is pre-eminently a political act by which people claim their right to potentialities that make prospects for a better future possible.

Waiting is not a static condition but rather a process and a practice. Waiting as wakeful navigation through material struggles in the present and 'directing one's mind toward' the not-yet, is a daily practice. For people who are constantly delayed and sent back to 'square one,' there is no end to waiting, but rather an endless struggle to withstand waiting and to demand change.

As I write these words, the world is witnessing a powerful *Black Lives Matter* movement in the United States and Europe—a growing anti-racism movement which has also become a mobilisation to force the former colonial countries to confront their racist histories.

The potentiality of the *Black Lives Matter* movement for political change is rooted in a profound ennui which is a result of a prolonged wait for justice. The awareness (boredom) that their waiting has not been defined by something (justice) that is yet to arrive, but rather by something that was never supposed to arrive, leads to the will to put an end to waiting—a radical will to unwait. Perhaps no one better that Martin Luther King expressed this radical unwaiting, who in his well-known letter written in a cell in Birmingham jail eloquently explained *why they can't wait*:

> For years now, I have heard the word "Wait!" It rings in the ear of every Negro with piercing familiarity. This "Wait" has almost always meant "Never." We must come to see, with one of our distinguished jurists, that "justice too long delayed is justice denied."[9]

---

9 Martin Luther King, *Why We Can't Wait* (New York: Penguin Group, 1964), 80–81.

Waiting for justice is assigned to those groups in society whose time is assumed to be less worth. The poor, racialised citizens, minorities, migrants, women, and prisoners all feel the weight of waiting on their shoulders more than others. The question is no longer what they are waiting for, but why they keep waiting for something that will never come.

Embedded in Neda's question, "did we suffer so much and for so long just for a piece of paper?" and refugee protests stuck by and between borders, and in the *Black Lives Matter* movements we can see a connectedness and continuum of experiences which are related to history and communities. The revolutionary potentiality in these instances is in the connectedness and the communicability of experiences. For Benjamin this transformation is when isolated experiences (*Erlebnis*) are linked to collective, accumulated, historical experiences (*Erfahrung*) and individual experiences are brought together and are historicised.[10] Martin Luther King's call for *unwaiting* is a call for all people for whom justice has been too long delayed and denied.

During the so-called 'refugee crisis' of 2015, hundreds of thousands of people crossed many borders on foot through the Balkans. Along the way they tuned train stations into bedrooms, train platforms into living rooms, abandoned carriages into kitchens, airport arrival and departure halls into waiting rooms, and walls into notebooks for messages and signs—leaving traces of themselves behind in the places they passed through. The following photographs (pp. 20-25) are taken in these places in search of remnants of hope; Idomeni, Lesbos, and Athens.

---

10 Walter Benjamin, "The Storyteller: Observations on the Works of Nikolai Leskov" in *Walter Benjamin: Selected Writings, Volume 3: 1935-1938* (Cambridge, MA: Harvard University Press, 2006).

The Weight of Waiting 25

Waiting

Faith Wilding

Waiting . . . waiting . . . waiting . . .
Waiting for someone to come in
Waiting for someone to hold me
Waiting for someone to feed me
Waiting for someone to change my diaper   Waiting . . .

Waiting to scrawl, to walk, waiting to talk
Waiting to be cuddled
Waiting for someone to take me outside
Waiting for someone to play with me
Waiting for someone to take me outside
Waiting for someone to read to me, dress me, tie my shoes
Waiting for Mommy to brush my hair
Waiting for her to curl my hair
Waiting to wear my frilly dress
Waiting to be a pretty girl
Waiting to grow up   Waiting . . .

Waiting for my breasts to develop
Waiting to wear a bra
Waiting to menstruate
Waiting to read forbidden books
Waiting to stop being clumsy

Waiting to have a good figure
Waiting for my first date
Waiting to have a boyfriend
Waiting to go to a party, to be asked to dance, to dance close
Waiting to be beautiful
Waiting for the secret
Waiting for life to begin   Waiting . . .

Waiting to be somebody
Waiting to wear makeup
Waiting for my pimples to go away
Waiting to wear lipstick, to wear high heels and stockings
Waiting to get dressed up, to shave my legs
Waiting to be pretty   Waiting . . .

Waiting for him to notice me, to call me
Waiting for him to ask me out
Waiting for him to pay attention to me
Waiting for him to fall in love with me
Waiting for him to kiss me, touch me, touch my breasts
Waiting for him to pass my house
Waiting for him to tell me I'm beautiful
Waiting for him to ask me to go steady
Waiting to neck, to make out, waiting to go all the way
Waiting to smoke, to drink, to stay out late
Waiting to be a woman   Waiting . . .
Waiting for my great love
Waiting for the perfect man
Waiting for Mr. Right   Waiting . . .

Waiting to get married
Waiting for my wedding day
Waiting for my wedding night
Waiting for sex

Waiting for him to make the first move
Waiting for him to excite me
Waiting for him to give me pleasure
Waiting for him to give me an orgasm   Waiting . . .
Waiting for him to come home, to fill my time   Waiting . . .
Waiting for my baby to come
Waiting for my belly to swell
Waiting for my breasts to fill with milk
Waiting to feel my baby move
Waiting for my legs to stop swelling
Waiting for the first contractions
Waiting for the contractions to end
Waiting for the head to emerge
Waiting for the first scream, the afterbirth
Waiting to hold my baby
Waiting for my baby to suck my milk
Waiting for my baby to stop crying
Waiting for my baby to sleep through the night
Waiting for my breasts to dry up
Waiting to get my figure back, for the stretch marks to go away
Waiting for some time to myself
Waiting to be beautiful again
Waiting for my child to go to school
Waiting for life to begin again   Waiting . . .

Waiting for my children to come home from school
Waiting for them to grow up, to leave home
Waiting to be myself
Waiting for excitement
Waiting for him to tell me something interesting, to ask me how I feel
Waiting for him to stop being crabby, reach for my hand, kiss me good morning
Waiting for fulfillment
Waiting for the children to marry

Waiting for something to happen   Waiting . . .
Waiting to lose weight
Waiting for the first gray hair
Waiting for menopause
Waiting to grow wise
Waiting . . .
Waiting for my body to break down, to get ugly
Waiting for my flesh to sag
Waiting for my breasts to shrivel up
Waiting for a visit from my children, for letters
Waiting for my friends to die
Waiting for my husband to die   Waiting . . .
Waiting to get sick
Waiting for things to get better
Waiting for winter to end
Waiting for the mirror to tell me that I'm old
Waiting for a good bowel movement
Waiting for the pain to go away
Waiting for the struggle to end
Waiting for release
Waiting for morning
Waiting for the end of the day
Waiting for sleep   Waiting . . .

"Waiting" was performed at Womanhouse in Los Angeles in 1972, sponsored by the Feminist Art Program, California Institute of the Arts.

Care to Wait

Jenny Richards and Gunilla Lundahl

Introduction

On a dark afternoon in late December, Jenny Richards arrives at the home of Gunilla Lundahl. She is greeted with homemade cinnamon biscuits and invited into a warm living room. In the room, a table is set for dinner. As they share the biscuits, they discuss what a gendered perspective on waiting might contribute to a critical understanding of what it means to wait. They begin by reciting Faith Wilding's poem *Waiting*, originally performed at the exhibition *Womanhouse* in Los Angeles in 1972, which describes the monotonous condition of waiting that is built into widespread female experience: "waiting for my breasts to develop," "waiting to get married," "waiting to get sick."[1] This seminal work brings to light how waiting is a disciplining force in a woman's life. Regardless of class or culture, women[2] are conditioned to wait resignedly for what might be described as the hallmarks of a heteronormative, middle-class life: marriage, babies, to be desirable to men. Yet, in the meantime, she does the work of maintaining the lives of those around her. Wilding draws attention to the assumption that a woman must wait for such things, rather than follow her desire. Or, if she dares, refuse the gendered narrative of waiting altogether. On this afternoon in December—a month in which many in Sweden,

---

[1] Faith Wilding, *Waiting*, 1972, Performance, 15 minutes.
[2] Please note that the authors use of *woman* or *women* is trans-inclusive.

irrespective of religion, *wait* for both the dark days to dwindle and for a winter break that might bring a fleeting pause in the ever-increasing workload that neoliberal racial capitalism[3] requires—Gunilla and Jenny discuss Faith Wilding's poem and how the act of waiting relates to their own research and experiences of feminist organising.

> **Gunilla:** Women's work particularly in relation to care work has often been improvised. You have to meet upcoming needs. You have to adapt to someone else. That breaks your own rhythm and scheduling and can cause waiting time. That's also the case when you have to follow another person's more structured patterns of work. Gendered work, particularly in relation to care, needs to be less structured as it is interrelated with other people's needs.[4]

> **Jenny:** Faith Wildings's piece develops a perspective on waiting in which a woman should fit into the narrative structure of a patriarchal system. It evokes a lot of 'shoulds'. I should get married, I should wear a bra. From this perspective, waiting is a way of both disciplining a woman's body and controlling the normative expectations she should have. The poem presents a figure of female subjectivity that is produced through the power structures of patriarchy; structures that invisibilise other forms of work and struggle and are dominated by what Paul B. Preciado would call the "old sexual regime," which is to say a regime in which sex is intrinsically linked to reproduction and based on an es-

---

3 Following Ruth Wilson Gilmore's work understanding that, "Capitalism requires inequality and racism enshrines it." See *Geographies of Racial Capitalism with Ruth Wilson Gilmore* directed by Kenton Card (An Antipode Foundation film ,2020), 1:42. https://www.youtube.com/watch?v=2CS627aKrJIble

4 "While there is nothing new in the entanglements of care with hegemonic regimes—one can only think of all the ways in which the caring mother is historically enthroned as much as confined and her caring body enlisted for the nation." Maria Puig de la Bellacasa, *Matters of Care: Speculative Ethics in More Than Human Worlds* (Minneapolis: University of Minnesota Press, 2017), 9.

sentialist gender binary.⁵ How have the expectations that Faith Wilding shares in her poem been fought against and reconstituted since the feminism of the 1970s? A movement that worked to redefine the role of women as reproducers of the workforce, what is valued as work and who is conceived as a worker, and the construction of the nuclear family.

Gunilla: Yes, and how that resistance and refusal operates between the lines of Faith Wilding's poem. Women have been forced to wait, but they have also resisted this position pushed upon them by reimagining waiting time for other doings, for imagining other desires and particularly for collective mobilising and organising. This side of waiting and its potential is not seen or valued by a patriarchal society. Kinds of resistance and refusal within everyday survival, types of activity that capitalism has made us blind to.

Jenny: Absolutely. Reimagining waiting can help us value and learn from practices that are continually marginalised in society, practices that are fighting against the weaponisation of waiting. The forms of waiting inflicted upon women as drawn out by Faith Wilding make me reflect on how the feminist movement from the 1970s was both a solace for many women and offered a kind of space of collective waiting to organise, learn, recuperate and resist. However, as I have learnt from you and others, we should remember that it was also a space that only included some forms of gendered waiting. European feminism from the so-called *Second Wave* of the 1970s is often historicised with an invariable lack of attention to intersectional practices and perspectives, and dominated by the experiences and challenges of middle-class white women. The work of scholar Françoise Vergès critically explores the centrality of whiteness within European feminism and the derad-

---

5 Paul B. Preciado, "Letter from a trans man to the old sexual regime," trans. Simon Pleasance, *Texte zur Kunst*, 22 Jan 2018, https://www.textezurkunst.de/articles/letter-trans-man-old-sexual-regime-paul-b-preciado

icalising of 1970s feminist work, exemplified in France where the fight for liberation became a fight for women's rights.[6] At the same time, feminised labour, characterised by its flexibility, responsiveness and adaptability,[7] was informing fast-developing processes of neoliberalisation of work and the workplace. The feminist desire to enter work as a tool for gaining equality with men is a notion based on the assumption that women were previously excluded from work, something referring largely to the experience of white middle-class women. Women of colour, women enslaved by colonial violence, and working-class women have been intensively incorporated into the workforce, often unpaid and subjected to its violent exploitation. While some of the hallmarks Faith Wilding is raising have thankfully been rejected by intersectional feminists and queer movements, many of these expectations have been reconstituted and still linger today. While you might not be waiting to have a boyfriend, the feeling of the *shoulds*—you *should* be doing this, or you *should* be doing that at a certain time in your life—is a component of waiting that is alive and well. Do you agree?

Gunilla: Yes. And this component of waiting is still very much alive in gendered work, as is the case with how care work is organised, particularly concerning what parts of care work you *should* pay attention

---

[6] See Françoise Vergès, *Le Ventre des Femmes: Capitalisme, Racialization, Féminisme* (Paris: Albin Michel, 2017) and Françoise Vergès, *Un Féminisme Decolonial* (Paris: La Fabrique, 2019).

[7] Feminisation of labour according to Angela Akorsu "has two dimensions. The first dimension refers to the quantitative increases in the number and proportion of females engaged in paid work over the last 20 or so years. The second dimension refers to flexible work forms such as home-based work, subcontracting, and part-time work, which, though not necessarily targeted at women and not necessarily bad, have attracted an increased number of women and have meant insecurity and precariousness of labor." Angela Akorsu, "Feminization of Labor" in *The Wiley Blackwell Encyclopedia of Gender and Sexuality Studies, Volume 5*, ed. Nancy Napes et. al (Hoboken NJ: Wiley-Blackwell, 2016), 1-3.

to. We have been reading together the poems of Linnea Swedenmark[8] where she describes how the essence of her work in home care is to respond to other people's needs. That means to listen and therefore also to wait. This type of work, as we have learnt from Linnea, becomes a form of mutual learning. But this part of care work, the essence of *what* you do, is invisible. It is impossible to account for. We can describe this part of the work as gendered, as throughout history this relational component has been invisibilised and devalued, because it is seldom described as work. What you are then paid for is just the technical work of describable tasks.

Jenny: So, waiting within care work can develop a space for collective pedagogy, complicating the binary between carer and cared for. This is important when we think about waiting within care work such as homecare, where care workers are paid to wait for people to eat their dinner. Or those receiving care who pay for workers to arrive at a specific time to prepare their breakfast. The way care work is organised mechanises and reduces care to a task of physical maintenance, eradicating the dimensions of care that Maria Puig de la Bellacasa identifies as involving "affect/affections and ethics/politics."[9] This can be seen in the schedules of home care workers built on 10 minute showers and 15 minute breakfasts that, as we have learnt from home care workers and know from doing these tasks ourselves, are impossible to quantify in these terms. The stipulation for care workers to care for more people in less time also diminishes the waiting time and thus the pedagogic and relational potential this time has. It is a way of ensuring the binary of carer and cared for is maintained and any human connection and alliance across this wage relation is limited.

---

8 Linnea Swedenmark, *En natt kidnappar jag alla mina hemtjänstkunder i en stulen buss* (Stockholm: Lil'Lit, 2020).
9 Puig de la Bellacasa, *Matters of Care: Speculative Ethics in More Than Human Worlds*, 5.

It makes me think about when my grandma was waiting on home care and she would get so cross when people were late. She believed that she should have a choice over how she was cared for. Like in all neoliberal societies, the notion of dependency is treated with contempt and twisted into a disciplining tool of punishment. In response, my grandma resisted the shame inflicted on those in need of care and fought to empower herself. But in this case, she ended up disciplining someone else, her home care worker, and reproducing the disciplining structures of care work that she herself was subject to. A more radical tactic for working against these power structures can be seen in how she developed very close friendships with some of her care workers. What do you think the artist Lilian Lindblad Domec, who also fought against this divisive dynamic and collaborated with her home care worker, would have said about waiting?

Gunilla: In terms of waiting, I think for Lilian time was always running, so she could hope for things to happen, but she would never wait for them. Lilian was a great artist with a huge capacity to use fantasy to escape the tough conditions she had to live under. She created her own worlds, there time was no problem, in her worlds she was the ruler of time. Together with her care worker, Thomas Gilek, they created a fake company called *Bolaget*[10] where they could depict the absurdity of contemporary life using the history of art. They created a language and mutual system of support that refused commercialised relations of care and how home care organises how you live your life and when you wait. They didn't have to wait for time together, time was constantly shared in their imaginations. When you can't resist the waiting time

---

10 Bolaget is a collaboration between Lilian Lindblad Domec and Thomas Gilek. Lindblad Domec (1922-2017) attended The Royal Academy of Art, Stockholm, in the 1940s. Her work includes painting, drawing, film, animation, stage design, ceramics, embroidery. Gilek (1968-2016) studied literature at Uppsala University and History of Ideas at Stockholm University. He worked as an assistant to Lindblad Domec for eight years.

pushed on you, you have to invent your own strategies to make the time meaningful for yourself. Women have good training in this.

Jenny: The act of being present also seems really important. Care work is highly skilled labour through which people have developed tools for paying close attention to the body, for listening to each other's bodies and emotions and not just what is communicated verbally through language. The importance of body knowledge makes me think of a conversation I had today with a friend with chronic fatigue about the knowledge developed when one is ill, and the problem with the idea of waiting in relation to illness. Waiting is impregnated with an idea that things will change after the waiting ends, but what if they don't? *Chronic* is derived from the Greek word *Chronos* which means 'of time,' and as the artist Joanna Hedva helps to clarify, "it specifically means 'a lifetime.'" So, a chronic illness is an illness that lasts a lifetime. In other words, it does not get better. There is no cure.[11] How does this disrupt the idea of *waiting to get better* and the normative binary between illness and health?

Gunilla: Yes, especially when waiting is systemic within the health care system. One evening, two weeks ago, I had a fall in the street near to a big hospital. I cut my face and was bleeding. I was accompanied to the entrance by a kind passer-by with the hope of finding someone to take care of my wounds. I was not quite so aware of the strong hierarchies in the care system. I was let in and made to wait six hours for the care I hoped for, yet never received. No one noticed my need for care. After about three hours of waiting a doctor sent me to have an X-ray and I was told to wait for the result. When the doctor popped by again, she said, "Your brain has been examined, there is nothing wrong, you can go home." I replied, "But my wounds?" The doctor then went on to say, "I am a doctor, I do not treat wounds; you should have gone to your local

---

11 Joanna Hedva, "Sick Woman Theory" in *Mask Magazine*, 2015, http://www.mask-magazine.com/not-again/struggle/sick-woman-theory

surgery." In this moment I felt deeply how my waiting was a form of punishment for having the pretension to ask for some of the doctor's precious time, in relation to what she deemed was a trivial problem. Waiting in the care system is effectively used to teach and underline the imbalance in the worth of the doctor's time and your time. It is a tool that demonstrates and reinforces hierarchical power structures.

Jenny: Absolutely, the lack of information and the assumption that you should inherently know how to navigate the healthcare system, which can feel deliberately complex, can make you feel vulnerable and exposed.

Gunilla: When I was waiting at the hospital for hours it made me think a lot about the architecture of the places we are forced to wait in . At that time, I entered two different waiting rooms. The first looked much like visiting a currency exchange office. In that waiting room you could wait for a number to give you passage into the next waiting room. The other was at a crossroads between two corridors. There you could find four rows of uncomfortable sofas, a coffee machine, a shelf with two old magazines, and a big TV screen with the volume up high. The TV isolated you from others and destroyed any potential for communing during that waiting time. The room was lit by a hard, bright light which spread evenly over this borderless environment. Waiting in such a place when you are feeling ill, or out of balance can be really destructive.

Jenny: I agree, it reminds me of a conversation with the artist Lisa Tan about a series of photographs she made of mass-reproduced images of artworks hanging in the waiting rooms of her psychologist and neurologist, some by famous artists such as Henri Matisse and Leonardo da Vinci. She says she thinks of the images as "circulating in art's hierarchies and value systems—and then getting stuck … [i]n the waiting room. With me."¹² These artworks were the companions she had to commune with during her waiting time, in this liminal moment, between paid professional care and the street outside. These rooms and moments of institutionalised waiting for care can so often be individualising and impersonal, which leads me to thinking how waiting could be collectivised. The interstitial moment of waiting seems to hold potential for communing with others, for learning about the power structures that we are inscribed in, for seeing what commonalities you share in your waiting with someone else. Working with Sophie Hope as part of *Manual Labours*, where we explore the impact of work on the body, we have found that commuting can be another form of waiting time, and that the space between work and home seems to hold some possibility.

Gunilla: It is interesting as I think people often say that waiting time is dead time. You can't use it for anything. But your comment makes me think of my time on the bus. When getting on the bus, you have the opportunity to decide whether this space gives you dead waiting time or if it has the possibility for interaction. As I am a person rich in age I can be looked at as a fairly friendly person, easy to address and so often people approach me. My bus time can be full of life. I think of the time of the commute as a time for the unexpected. A place for meetings.

Jenny: True, especially if you are lucky enough to meet people who are not glued to their smart phones (as sadly I often am). I was reading a text by the artist Carolyn Lazard who talks about how "the advent of the smartphone has usurped leisure time from the working able-bodied."¹³ She points to how the phone allows us to be accessible, effective at all hours. So, in fact, the commute for many is an extension of their

---

12 Lisa Tan, *My Pictures of You*, Text from Exhibition at Galleri Riis, 2019, accessed May 29, 2020, https://lisatan.net/current-work.html

13 Carolyn Lazard, "How to Be a Person in the Age of Autoimmunity" in *Cluster*, 2013.

working day, which often cuts off the potential that this waiting time might offer.

Gunilla: Yes, the role of the telephone has been critical in the transformation of waiting. The precarity of not knowing when you are on or off work confuses the concept of waiting time. It creates a sense of insecurity, but one altogether different to the violent insecurity of waiting time for people who have migrated to Europe and await their residency permit. Agency over this waiting time is brutally prevented. The lack of information, irrational communication and racist policies create a particularly calculated and aggressive form of subjection to waiting.

Jenny: There are so many different ways in which forms of power and waiting intersect. Is being able to wait for someone or something a privilege and does it say something about how much autonomy you have over your time? Who can afford to wait today? How does never having to wait pertain to the celebrated, elite group of workers jetting around the world and what bodies make this type of work possible? The cleaners of offices and those workers in hospitality and care whose job is to *wait on* others. The racial and class distinction between workers who are forced to wait and those that appear to never be able to wait is important to critically examine.[14]

Gunilla: Absolutely, the distinction between the performing body *who has no time to wait* and the invisibilised body who is made *to wait* in order to respond and support this body is crucial and highlights the oppressive conditions of much caring work. Yet, within this power structure we can take on another perspective; what is possible to achieve and resist within this waiting time? How might you be able to foster

---

14 On the distinction between the white male performing body and the racialised, invisiblised female body, see Françoise Vergès, "Capitalocene, Waste, Race, and Gender" in *e-flux*, no. 100, 2019, https://www.e-flux.com/journal/100/269165/capitalocene-waste-race-and-gender

your imagination and fantasy within the waiting time inherent in jobs that involve the care of others? Something women in particular have been creatively engaged with for centuries. In structured time there is not much chance left for letting new ideas in, not so much chance to invigorate ideas and imagination that could shake these existing structures of gendered and racialised exploitation that we have been discussing. I am thinking about how waiting time can be creative.

Jenny: This makes me think about organising in spaces of waiting. Many people I have met in feminist and activist communities who are forced into a situation of waiting use this time for arranging collective activities. They initiate study groups, parties and coffee clubs, which often become spaces for developing more overt forms of resistance, such as campaigns, mutual aid funds and collective care schedules. They refuse alienating patterns of waiting and instead mobilise in order to challenge the oppressive structural conditions they face. It also reminds me of the numerous self-organised collective kitchens that have sprung up in various political contexts. As architect and researcher Anna Puigjaner has shown, they provide care and support for social movements, address food poverty in periods of economic and labour insecurity and become spaces of politicisation and community. Some of the kitchens that were set up in Lima in the late 1970s to support communities that struggled against the military regime still continue today.[15]

Gunilla: Yes, which points my mind towards another aspect of waiting, which can be very respectful; I am going to wait for you to be ready to share something, I am going to wait for you to be ready to do something. In this way waiting can be negotiated as a supportive agreement

---

15 Anna Puigjaner, "Bringing the Kitchen Out of the House." in *eflux Architecture*, 2019, https://www.e-flux.com/architecture/overgrowth/221624/bringing-the-kitchen-out-of-the-house/

that enables people to have time. An interrelated type of waiting, in which you are waiting for each other.

Jenny: As you brought up earlier, waiting is so dependent on what position you have in society. If you are someone who has a lot of control over your time, and someone makes you wait, it can become a pedagogical space. You might be encouraged to question your impatience and ask why you view your time as more valuable than others'. This makes me think of collaboration, in which a shared temporality is created. Working collaboratively necessitates waiting as one can't always decide when things happen. Everyone works at different speeds, has different capacities and commitments, different responsibilities, different privileges, and collaboration needs to acknowledge and work with these, it needs its own collective time. There is a lot to learn from the waiting involved in this process, particularly regarding expectations of work and how they are internalised and embodied. For example, in the cultural sector the expectation of constant production is endemic; being made to slow down and wait brings these normalised and embodied logics into sharp relief. Collaboration asks you to wait for each other as you describe, regardless of what deadlines are imposed upon your individual work. This is something I constantly struggle with when working collaboratively within the context of an educational institution. Here you see a clash of two different structures: the academy and its focus on the individual, results and deadlines and the improvised and ongoing, process-led way of working in collaboration with others. What I love about collaboration is that the need to create collective time not only creates a space for you to reflect on the logics underpinning how you work, but also demands that you transform how you work. Through this, the possibility for self-transformation opens up.

Gunilla: What is interesting for me in waiting is that waiting is a moment that teaches us to slow down and reflect.[16] As we've noted, waiting can become a pedagogical space, a way to teach yourself to be present. The logic of waiting often presumes that you want to be somewhere else, somewhere ahead, in the next job, the next relationship. But using waiting time as a way to learn how to be present can maybe circumvent this tendency. What new things can we hear in being slow? I am thinking about the time of pregnancy. You are planning, but you don't know exactly what you are planning for. You become open to things that can also trigger your fantasies and enrich your well-being. During pregnancy your body is also waiting and preparing and becomes sensitively aware of what this means. In many ways, your body is taken out of your control and you must wait and listen. The writer Arundhati Roy has put this idea in words that inspire me: "Another world is not only possible, she is on her way. On a quiet day, I can hear her breathing."[17]

Jenny: And maybe that new world, as we often discuss, is one that centres care, not as something you wait for, but something that is lived and breathed within everything we do. Rather than a waiting with no end, what about putting into practice caring that has no end? This perspective could contribute to dismantling the current system of oppression and violence as we know it. As Joanna Hedva writes: "The most anti-capitalist protest is to care for another and to care for yourself. To take on the historically feminised and therefore invisible practice of nursing, nurturing, caring."[18]

---

16 Nataša Petrešin-Bachelez calls for 'an invitation for curators operating in distinct geographies but within an intertwined geopolitical reality to slow down their ways of working and being, to imagine new ecologies of care as a continuous practice of support, and to listen with attention to feelings that arise from encounters with objects and subjects.' Nataša Petrešin-Bachelez "For Slow Institutions." in *e-flux journal* #85, 2017, https://www.e-flux.com/journal/85/155520/for-slow-institutions
17 Arundhati Roy at the World Social Forum, Porto Allegre, Brazil, 2003.
18 Hedva, "Sick Woman Theory."

A buzzer goes. Gunilla gets up and heads to the kitchen, while Jenny presses stop on the sound recorder. Their waiting for dinner together is over.

Afterword

In 2007, over 30 years since Faith Wilding made *Waiting*, she was invited to share the work as part of a major exhibition of 1970s feminist art called *Wack! Art and the Feminist Revolution* at the Museum of Contemporary Art, Los Angeles. She accepted the invitation on the premise that she would remake the performance from her perspective in 2007. Within our conversation the theme of reimagining and collectivising waiting time as a space for learning and organising connected to how Wilding developed this new performance. In her remake, called *Wait-With*[19] Wilding moved away from a performance that exposed patriarchal subjugation, where waiting is "a kind of enforced passivity, towards waiting as a condition that is connected to activist resistance and political action. Waiting understood as a refusal to act or produce."[20]

Since this conversation in December 2019 the world has become a very different place. What Shahram Khosravi describes as a *global waithood* has developed, a condition produced by the worldwide pandemic of COVID-19. Waiting to touch people again, waiting for a vaccine, waiting for social security for those whose jobs are lost, waiting to return to work, waiting for work to return to 'normal,' waiting for protective clothing, waiting for politicians to stop bailing out banks and invest in healthcare, waiting to be together. Without the possibility of seeing each other in person, we speak to each other daily by telephone, each in our separate homes. Being forced to stay at home and avoid social interaction has, for us, engendered new relations toward

---

19 Faith Wilding, *Wait-With*, 2007, Performance.
20 Amelia Jones, "Faith Wilding and Wait-With" in *Perform, Repeat, Record: Live History* (Bristol: Intellect, 2012), 253-254.

work, time, imagination and care. Yet, while we have the privilege to be at home, to still work from home, many do not. Many expose themselves to high risks in facing the challenge of making enough money for rent and food. Our telephone call is a call to check in with each other, to see how we are and examine how this challenging moment is affecting others and ourselves in very different ways. It has made us ask ourselves how to collaborate under conditions of isolation. With days merging into days, time feels closer, you listen to your body, how do I feel today? You listen to each other, how are you today? You become closer to what it takes to sustain yourself and others. You try to enrich your social body with online conversations. Your dreams become more intense each night. From isolation you try to find ways to support care workers and those in need of care.

Reading this text now brings some of our ideas around the potential of waiting as a space of pedagogy into new light. Our experience of confinement connects to our discussions on the importance of imagination as a prefigurative tool for change. Imagination is a rich resource that we perhaps don't pay enough attention to. It has also laid bare the ableist assumptions and exclusionary structures much cultural and collective work is predicated upon. Many talk of getting back to 'normal' but as we have learnt during this waithood that we have shared together, returning to business as usual would be to ignore the profound inequalities, violence and exploitation that racial capitalism is built upon. The pandemic has further exposed the distinction between those undervalued bodies who take care of society and bear the most risk, and those bodies that society values and protects. This waiting time we have shared urgently reaffirms that our task is to continue to politicise care work; to centre our interdependent care needs and vulnerabilities in a world that is determined to marginalise them. To use this waiting time, as feminists before us have taught, for imagining and organising, for listening and learning, for caring. We are not waiting or willing to go back to business as usual and the promotion of more uncaring worlds.

Lisa Tan, "Waiting Room of a Psychologist" (Henri Matisse, Cup of Oranges, 1916) 144 x 164 x 4 cm and "Waiting Room of a Psychologist" (John Wipp, Blåe) 144 x 129 x 4 cm. 2019. Installation View. Pigment print on acid free cotton paper. Photo:Adrian Bugge.
Images courtesy and © the artist.

This Sea is Mohammad al-Khatib's

Adania Shibli

But who is Mohammad al-Khatib? We know he is a young man, twenty years old, and that he is from al-Khalil. And he wanted to go to the sea, with his friends. We can then assume that he deliberated at length over the question; how to get there? We can imagine, under the present circumstances, two possibilities of a sea that Mohammad al-Khatib can visit.

The first possibility is the sea of Gaza. As its name quite literally indicates, the sea of Gaza can be accessed at the moment only by whoever finds themselves there. And how can Mohammad al-Khatib get there? He first needs to reach Allenby Bridge in order to cross the Israeli-controlled borders to Jordan, and so do his friends, one of whom is denied entry to Jordan by Israeli intelligence, then they should head to Amman airport, and from there, to Cairo airport. But before that, Mohammad al-Khatib needs to obtain a visa to enter Egypt, which is very difficult to get, but he can try nonetheless, and he does, and so do his friends, except for one who is on the Egyptian intelligence list. From Cairo, he will head to al-Arish, except for his friend who is denied entry to Egypt, despite having a visa, since he was unfriendly to the security services. There he will arrive in Rafah, where he will find the crossing closed and will be ordered to go back to where he came from.

But then he might find someone to take him to Gaza through the tunnels, and from there to the sea; something that is getting more and more difficult to do these days, since the Egyptian authorities waged their US-and Israeli-supported war against tunnels leading to Gaza. And so, after three days travelling, Mohammad al-Khatib will arrive, without any of his friends, at the sea of Gaza, on the first of September 2016 at around five in the afternoon, and will have one hour before the night falls and with it the Israeli naval artillery. But that hour with the sea is what counts. It counts sixty minutes, or three thousand and six hundred seconds; an infinite time. Who has ever counted up to the number 3600, except for the waves of the sea?

The second possibility is the sea of Yafa. And to get there, we can imagine under the present circumstances, two possibilities. The first possibility is that Mohammad al-Khatib's father, or his uncle or his cousin, or a close friend of one of these, or a close friend of an acquaintance of theirs, has a connection to someone who has a high position at one of the Palestinian Authority offices, or is an informer of the lowest degree and is providing Israeli intelligence with information. That connection got Mohammad al-Khatib a permit to enter Israeli-controlled territories, except for area D, from 7am until 7pm, which allows him to visit the sea. What about his friends? Well, they are his friends, and they too got a permit, except for one who is on the Palestinian intelligence list. That day, the first of September 2016, they all start early and are the first to stand at the Bethlehem checkpoint. They were delayed a bit, and one was turned back for no reason, but at around five in the afternoon, after having been stopped here, searched there, with one arrested here, and another one arrested there, Mohammad al-Khatib arrived alone at the sea of Yafa; a name which is not quite literal, but metaphorical, since Yafa is many kilometres away. He has one full hour, leaving one hour for the road before his permit expires. But that hour with the sea is what counts. It counts sixty minutes, or three thousand and six hundred seconds; an infinite time. Who has ever counted up to the number 3600, except for the waves of the sea?

The second possibility is that Mohammad al-Khatib's father died, and so did his uncle, his cousin, their close friend, and the acquaintance of a close friend with a connection to someone who has a high position at one of the Palestinian Authority offices, or had been an informer of the lowest degree and provided the Israeli intelligence with information, who also died a while ago; but not the son of his neighbours, who needed none of these connections to reach 'inside'. He works there without a permit, and he knows how to get there without a permit. Mohammad al-Khatib spends all night with the neighbours' son in order to learn the *illegal* route that will allow him to get to the sea.

And we can imagine under the present circumstances, two possibilities for an illegal route. The first possibility is to drive a car with a yellow number plate. Mohammad al-Khatib has a friend with such a car and with a desire to go to the sea. He leaves, with his friends, except for one as there was not enough space in the car, early in the morning from al-Khalil to Wadi an-Nar, or the Fire Valley way, until they reach Beit Jala, except for one who gets carsick due to the many turns and curves for which Wadi an-Nar is known. They pull out their sunglasses and kippas, and head to the tunnel checkpoint just as the rush hour hits, with the settlers of the south on the road for work in Jerusalem. And since the soldiers don't want to disturb any of the settlers, or delay them, the car passes; alas half way to the sea, the car gets hot, and after a couple of hours trying to cool it but failing, the friend driving and another friend stay behind with it, and Mohammad al-Khatib rides the buses to the sea. He arrives at around five in the afternoon on the first of September 2016, and he has one full hour before he needs to ride the buses back to al-Khalil during the rush hour when his chances of going unnoticed are higher. But that hour with the sea is what counts. It counts sixty minutes, or three thousand and six hundred seconds; an infinite time. Who has ever counted up to the number 3600, except for the waves of the sea?

The second possibility is not finding a friend with a car with a yellow number plate in the entire area of al-Khalil, so that Mohammad al-Khatib, with his friends, need to use the on-foot illegal route to get to the sea.

He prepares himself, along with his friends, to leave before the dawn rises. He heads to the south, rather than the north, to the area of al-Ramadin. There, between the hills, passes the route of the wall, still incomplete, in the form of wired fences. They get out of the rented car, and run to the fence, and run and run, all reaching it except for one friend, who loses a shoe as they run, and goes back to look for it. Then, as they jump down from the fence, another friend tears his jeans all the way from his thighs to his bottom, with blood gushing out, and he is left behind. Mohammad al-Khatib cannot be delayed, otherwise they will be caught, and he keeps running until he reaches the small white bus with a driver from Rahat, waiting with the doors wide open, and once Mohammad al-Khatib enters, he leaves the scene at full speed. But the price is high, and Mohammad al-Khatib only has money for the first third of the journey. With no money left, he hitchhikes to the sea, where he arrives at around five in the afternoon on the first of September 2016, and he has one full hour before he needs to hitchhike back to al-Khalil. But that hour with the sea is what counts. It counts sixty minutes, or three thousand and six hundred seconds; an infinite time. Who has ever counted up to the number 3600, except for the waves of the sea?

And there he is standing before the sea, where he may finally shout out loud: "This sea is mine."

And we can imagine under the present circumstances, two possibilities for a response from the sea. The first possibility is that the sea, upon hearing Mohammad al-Khatib's shouts (in Arabic obviously) and glimpsing in his raised hands as he ran towards it what may resemble a knife, it panicked. The sea thought Mohammad al-Khatib wanted to stab it. The news of young men from al-Kahlil who had been suspected of planning knife attacks are too many for the sea to be cool about it. The sea calls the police to inform it about this shouting and running man. But prior to the police's arrival and as time was still running, as was Mohammad al-Khatib, the sea jumps up to neutralise him, and pulls him to the ground and drags him under to contain the threat. But misfortune happens and Mohammad al-Khatib dies in the process.

The second possibility is that the sea, upon hearing Mohammad al-Khatib's shouts (in Arabic obviously), opens its heart, since this is the sea of Yafa and it has not heard Arabic at this spot for a long time, and maybe it glimpses in the raised hands of Mohammad al-Khatib as he runs towards it the hug he intends to give it. Like a lover's ear and eye, the sea does not confuse what its beloved says for the opposite. But like in love stories, once one claims another is theirs, the other is bound to claim the same.

As the sea hears Mohammad al-Khatib shouting, "this sea is mine," it calls back, "you are mine." And the sea does not let go of Mohammad al-Khatib ever again.

Sandhours

Majd Abdel Hamid

> Time is the dimension of decay and resistance, of dissolution and of re-composition. Time is the process of becoming other of every fragment in every other fragment, forever.
>
> Franco 'Bifo' Berardi, *Futurability*[1]

Recognition of the hourglass as a symbol of time has survived its obsolescence as a timekeeper. Unlike most other methods of measuring time, the hourglass concretely represents the present as being between the past and the future, and this has made it an enduring symbol of time itself. The powder in each hourglass consists of crushed cement bits chipped from *the Wall* in the West Bank mixed with sand grains. The Hourglasses are handmade and produced in collaboration with a glass factory in Hizma—a Palestinian town in the Jerusalem Governorate, located half a kilometre Northeast of Jerusalem city.

The following images (pp. 58-62) are from Majd Abdel Hamid's work "Hourglasses" 2012. Images courtesy and © the artist.

---

[1] Franco 'Bifo' Berardi, *Futurability* (London: Verso, 2019).

Stolen Time

Shahram Khosravi

I.

The long queues outside the embassies of the rich countries in the capitals of poor countries; the long queues of travellers without documents along European borders or along the Mexico-United States border; the queues of refugees in Dadaab camp in Kenya or Zaatari camp in Jordan; the never-ending queues inside the Australian detention centres on Manus Island; all these queues are paradigmatic images of our time, an unequal world; showing who is waiting and who imposes waiting on others.

    Keeping people in prolonged waiting is a technique to delay them. Delaying is a technique of domination, making the other's time seem less worthy. No one better than a migrant can testify to it. The journey from Milan to Rome by train takes about four hours. For Hamid it took two weeks, since he was recurrently stopped, controlled, and forced to get off the train. The distance between the Greek-Turkish border and Komotini, a small Greek town, is around 100 km. Ahmad walked that distance 16 times—15 times he was deported back to Turkey. For Mohamad, the journey from Athens to Berlin took two years and for Sara the journey from Kurdistan to Amsterdam took 15 years.

'Killing time' is conducted by those who impose waiting.

II.

The main purpose of delaying a migrant at the border is to remind her of her place in the racial hierarchy. A migrant from the Global South, particularly if she is from a former colonised country, has to be delayed because she, as the antithesis to what Europe is supposed to be, has historically been imagined so.

For Frantz Fanon colonial racism is built on the idea of the belatedness of non-Europeans. A black person, a non-European, a colonised person arrives to white time, and it is already too late. She arrives to a pre-existing world of meanings, a world already shaped, in which a non-European is not a subject with a history and agency but is only an object, fixed as a category and imagined in a different temporality.[1]

Part of the colonial condition is the racialisation of time. Racialisation of time means *the other* arrives to a world in which bodies are already divided. A world where access to resources and power is allocated according to this logic of belatedness. To a *white time* that is assumed and presented as secular, civilised, modern, progressive, neutral, the racialised other always arrives too late. She is assumed to be stuck in a historical belatedness, or as Dipesh Chakrabarty put it, in the "waiting room of history,"[2] and therefore regarded and treated as unequal.

The historical belatedness turns the migrant not into a *foreigner*, but rather into an inexplicable *stranger*. The logic of belatedness makes the migrant unknowable and pushes everything about her and around her towards the impossibility of understanding.

---

1 Frantz Fanon, *Black Skin, White Masks*, (New York: Grove Press, 1967), 122.
2 Dipesh Chakrabarty *Provincializing Europe: Postcolonial Thought and Historical Difference* (Princeton, N.J.: Princeton University Press, 2000).

III.

A common experience of being constantly delayed and kept in waiting is a sense of being sent back in time, expressed in terms of being sent 'back to square one.' Back in square one and you have to start from scratch again, and again, and again. People are sent back and forth between reception camps and removal camps, between asylum seeking and deportability, between countries, between legislations, between institutions, and between periods of waiting. One basic rationale for this temporal bordering (waiting, delaying and circulating) is the belief that the time of these people is less worthy than the time of citizens.

In this condition of circulation, of being exposed to constant delaying, one never gets the chance to finalise anything; to complete an education or a training program, to get involved and participate politically and socially in new societies, to see their children grow up, or to build a loving relationship. Migrants are kept in circulation, so their experience is usually an experience of *not arriving*, an experience of being temporary, and of being constantly delayed.

Keeping people in prolonged waiting, constantly delaying them, and repeatedly sending them back to square one, generates a large amount of surplus time. A crucial question is who controls and possesses this time.

Migrants' time is not killed, but rather stolen.

Stealing time becomes even more explicit in the case of detention and deportation. When people are spatially removed, they are automatically robbed of amounts of time. The time people have spent to accumulate economic, social and cultural capital is taken away by detention and deportation.

How much time has been stolen?

In the case of those who had permission to work before being exposed to deportation—what about taxes and social security contributions people have paid before being removed? What about unused holidays? How much money did their employers save in the form of unpaid wages? How much money does the state save in the form of unpaid pensions? How much surplus value has been produced for the capitalists through deportation globally? How many working hours are stolen?

The extra value added to commodities comes from unpaid time, that is stolen time. Similar to the case of colonial extraction, temporal bordering is nothing but an act of stealing—the theft of time.

Today's border practices are not different from yesterday's colonial practices. While colonial capitalism turned lands into wastelands to plunder the wealth underneath, border practices turn migrants' time into waste time to steal their labour. The current border regime that keeps migrants in prolonged waiting and constantly delays them is part of a larger and older project of colonial accumulation by dispossession and expulsion, stealing wealth, labour and time.

Today as yesterday, her land and her time are stolen, only because she is told that she has arrived too late. Much too late.

Undocumented:
The Architecture of Migrant Detention

Tings Chak

Undocumented: The Architecture of Migrant Detention documents the banality and violence of the architecture in contrast to the stories of daily resistance among immigration detainees. Migrants are detained primarily because they are undocumented. Likewise, these sites of detention bare little trace—drawings and photos are classified; access is extremely limited. The detention centres, too, are undocumented. This book explores migrant detention centres in Canada, an important sector of the Global North's prison industrial complex, and questions the role of architectural design in the control and management of migrant bodies in such spaces. Using the conventional architectural tools of representation, I situate, spatialise, and confront the silenced voices of those who are detained and the anonymous individuals who design spaces of confinement.

The following illustrations (pp. 72-78) are an excerpt from Tings Chak's book "Undocumented: the Architecture of Migrant Detention" published by The Architecture Observer (Amsterdam/Montreal, 2014).

Tings Chak

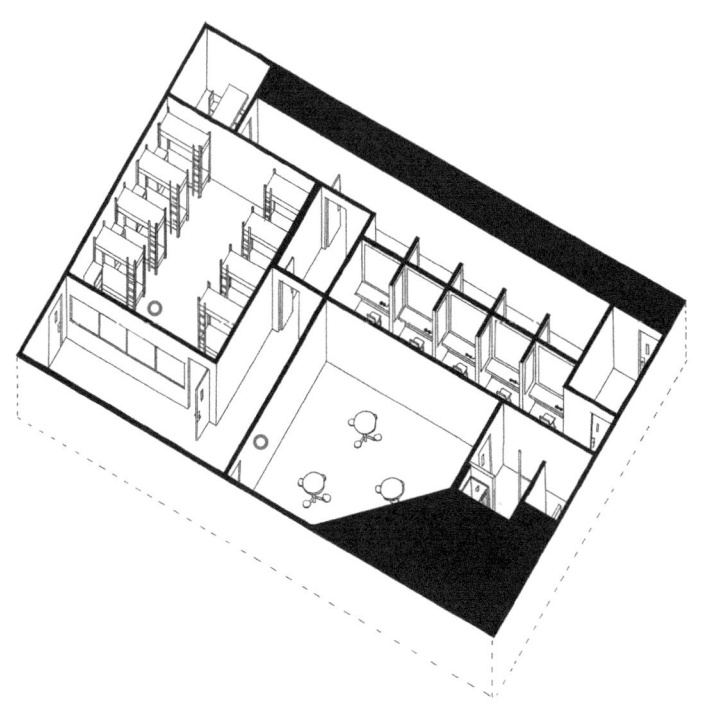

Undocumented: The Architecture of Migrant Detention 73

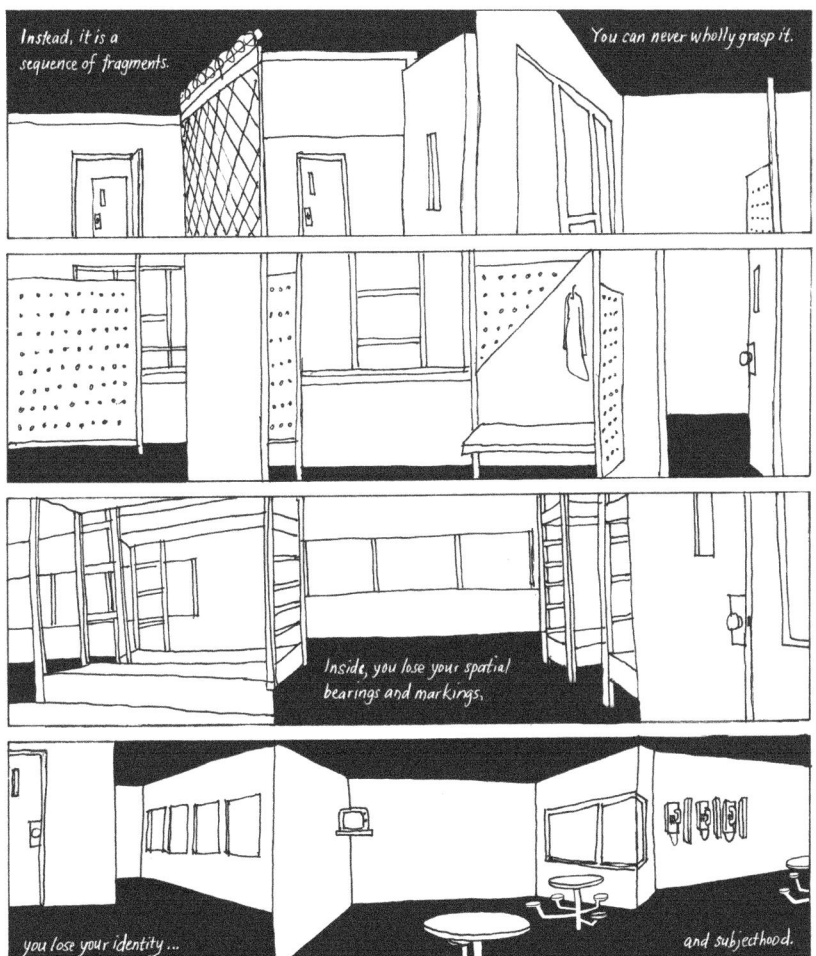

The minimum habitable space for an incarcerated individual is measured.

   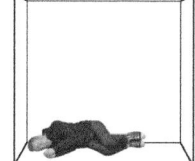

2 square metres of floor area

  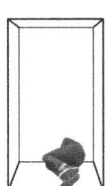   

and 3.5 cubic metre of air space.

In this volume, the contents of your life are caged. But every human action cannot be programmed or predicted, our bodies always find ways to carve out space, to refocus our attention from the geometry to the lived experience, from the container to the contained.

Undocumented: The Architecture of Migrant Detention

There is an immigration detainee on hunger strike for over sixty days in protest of indefinite detention. Held for 28 months in a maximum security prison without charge or trial, he said, "I missed three of my son's birthdays, I missed three anniversaries with my wife... I cannot see myself here being detained indefinitely and thinking about them. That will drive me crazy. So I have to keep it out of sight and out of mind. How inhumane is that?"

"I am a father and I am a husband."

"Should I even be allowed to feel like this?"

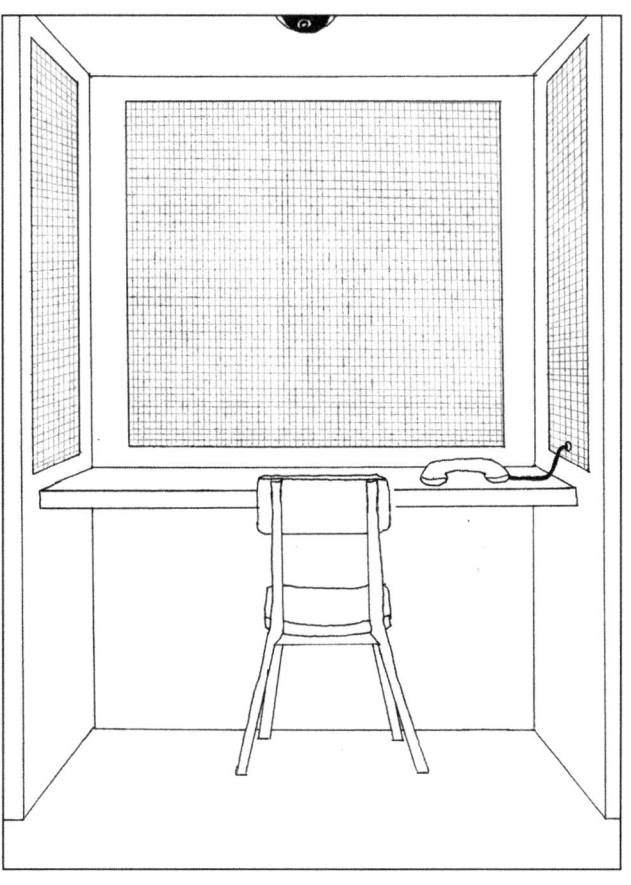

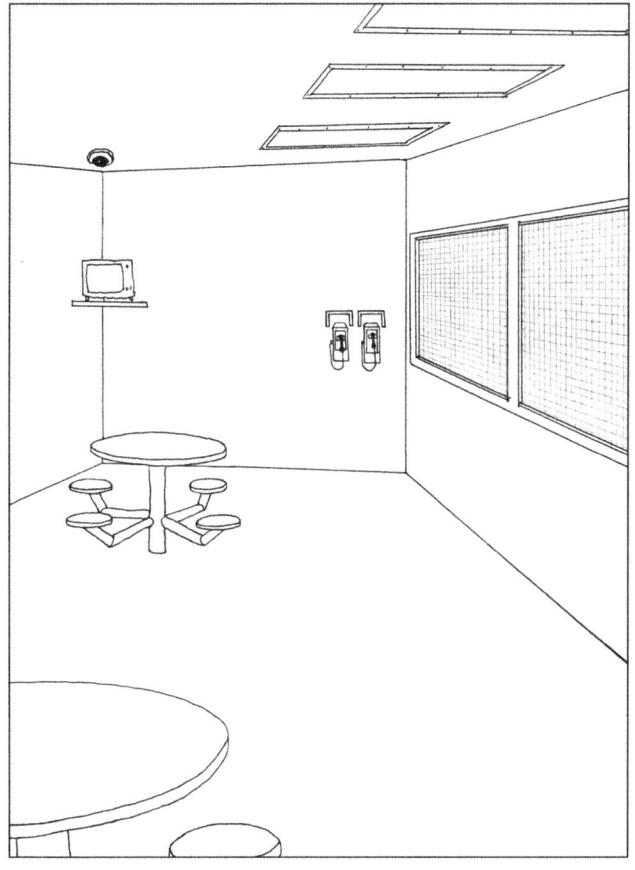

Remain

Hoda Afshar

Remain was made in collaboration with several of the men who still [2018] remain on Manus Island, Papua New Guinea, six or more years after they left their homelands to seek asylum in Australia, but instead were sent to languish in the remote offshore detention centre. Comprising still and moving images, voice recordings and text, the work involves these men retelling their individual and shared stories through staged images, words, and poetry, and bearing witness to life in the Manus camps: from the death of friends and dreams of freedom, to the strange air of beauty, boredom, and violence that surrounds them on the island.

The following images (pp. 82-87) are stills from Hoda Afshar's video work "Remain, 2018" 2-channel digital video, colour, sound. Images courtesy and © the artist and Milani Gallery, Brisbane.

Remain 83

Remain 87

Arriving to Depart

Omid Tofighian

Departure gates dictate an exceptional kind of order—arriving to leave, inauguration and closure, a beginning and an end. Waiting at the gate is part of a traveller's ritual. A borderland, the departure gate embodies many perplexities. Sydney Airport's runways encroach onto Botany Bay. A frightening monument to intrusion constructed by settlers, every day is marked by arrivals, colonial reminders of an incursion on the same 1788 site of colonial violence, every day is now marked by departures, but leaving from the airport functions within the narrative of that earlier arrival, a paradoxical performance enacted on this border. European invaders named the location after one of the oldest branches of science. But botany is not just a way of categorising, studying and controlling; especially for First Nations, botany is associated with healing. Borders embody paradox.

Travelling creates uncanny tensions. Before flying out I always think I am going to experience some major problem. Will I be caught up in traffic or will there be a train delay? Have I forgotten my passport? Did I book my flight correctly, did I check if I received confirmation? While travelling to the airport this same feeling morphs in different ways until I actually take off. Waiting begins early on during a trip. When does this anticipation actually begin? Does it have a definite beginning and end? When I am finally at the departure gate, I wonder to myself how I ever made it there, did that just work out? I am here now, waiting for my flight. But really, the signs are clear if I read them correctly; they always tell me that there's little chance of anything going wrong. I am fine, as long as I wait at consecutive intervals and according to a ceremonial order. Travelling makes you an augur.

On the way to Sydney Airport the city somehow seems both sparse and brimming with entities. Trees grab at street signs, traffic lights throw messages for passers-by, buildings of oscillating heights drape clusters of suburban locals and watchful birds. Interpreting the best course of action when departing requires interpreting some kind of 'divine will.' *Reading signs*. Understanding how best to depart means *reading* one's passport, visas, previous travel experiences, the direction of travel paths, and the places and emotions along the way. Like all rituals, engaging in travel produces its own signs for appropriate action, these are clear to those already initiated. That is, those with documents that enable smooth passage, documents that embody power—minimal or no waiting, peaceful and memorable departure, warm and confident arrival. The authorities know that the way one travels can affect order, so they only lead and support the initiated. I have passed the rite of passage and so I carry the mark. My passport. With it I embody that power.

Waiting for me is only an interval, not a conviction. I simply wait at this border before I can cross many others. I contrast this with the borderlands Australia has created elsewhere which function as purgatory—similar to how this island was invaded and used as a location for multiple and multiplying prison systems. Australia has overtaken islands and their surrounding waters for colonial exploit—Manus Island (in Papua New Guinea) and Nauru are sites where people seeking asylum wait without end, where they are indefinitely detained in carceral sites, judged without clear and just laws, where they are categorised between animal and human, herded and counted like animals but also with unique numbers that distinguish them as individuals, this way they can be more easily punished and forced to wait for more punishment while the authorities deflect scrutiny and act with impunity. These islands are former colonies run by a logic that dictates oppression, domination and subjugation, where vulnerable people wait in immigration detention according to a colonial logic and without any routes of escape.

Airports are liminal zones, but they are not purgatory like Manus Island. I know this distinction well due to direct contact with border crossers just like me; however, my friends incarcerated in Manus are uninitiated travellers for whom waiting has a totally different meaning. The only thing that is on time in the detention system is systematic torture; the detention industry is a factory of affliction. Here at Sydney Airport I am forced to engage in another kind of waiting—I am expecting an urgent text message from Manus Island regarding another horrific incident.

I follow the maps endowed by the system, so I am rewarded with signs along my way. I have arrived, and I am ready to depart. Check-in, security clearance, passport control, gate lounge. At the gate people sit waiting to board. I notice a few holding their passports—the colours are different to mine. Australian passports are navy blue, I see some with red, black and green. A mother and daughter are in conversation, but I am inattentive, so much so that the topic does not even register, let alone the language they speak. I look to see if the text message has arrived—I am still waiting. I reflect on the queue at the coffee shop, it is fast and cheerful as travellers move through. I turn to view the rows of white planes lined up waiting on the tarmac, they glow with the certainty of a safe departure. I look up to gaze at another plane arriving in Sydney containing passengers waiting to land, a perpetual ritual of arrival and departure and a cascade of signs, overflowing signs of movement, signs of waiting, acts of traversing, a carousel of power and autonomy.

I'm still waiting for the text message. Everyone is waiting here, but everyone is moving. Every now and then I fumble through my things to check that I have what I need for this trip. I intermittently reach into my jacket pocket to touch my passport. I know it is there, but I want to reassure myself. I remember on some trips I would reach for it in the same pocket and my heart stopped for a second—but then I remembered that I had either put it in my bag or in another pocket. I do not even need to see it now; I just touch it to simply reinforce its significance. I know well its texture and size. I feel reassured knowing that things are on my side.

Waiting here conjures up memories of similar circumstances, I recall the first time I departed from Cairo Airport. Like all my experiences when travelling to an airport I always felt something was going to go wrong along the way, but I arrived after waiting some time in traffic. I have never been asked to show my passport when entering an airport, but there I was stopped with a number of others on arrival. I reached into my pocket but could not feel my passport, I searched other pockets and still could not feel it. I was denied entry and made to stand on the side of a busy footpath, inconveniencing the rushing travellers as I rummaged through my bags, I was causing suspicion. I am initiated, I thought! I have never had to manage this problem. I found my passport, power was restored. It was a moment of exclusion, even though I found my passport I realised I was not accepted as an auger and I could not read the signs for border crossers here, what I had been trained to do was not enough, I could not understand why this ritual was different. However, I still could not enter the airport. The guard also required a printed flight ticket—the signs were clearly ambiguous to me. After some explanation and opening up a vague email using my phone I was hastily ushered in; actually, the guard was more annoyed and did not even look at my evidence. I had to negotiate the ticket problem all over again when going through the metal detectors before check-in—misunderstanding codes is always imminent when one is uninitiated.

The signs are clear for me here at Sydney Airport. After I feel my passport in my pocket and confirm its presence I try to disconnect and think about nothing. But ideas and stories travel too and at the departure gate I am like a receptacle. I quickly scroll my Facebook feed and also check my WhatsApp messages (nothing yet). Various advertisements related to the airport appear. The first thing that sparks my interest is something related to the name of the airport. Sydney airport is named after a guy called Kingsford Smith. I google his name—I never cared one bit who he was until now. My curiosity is aroused for some reason. He is also represented on an old version of Australian currency.

Sir Charles Kingsford Smith is renowned for crossing borders. He was the first to cross between the United States and Australia and between Australia and New Zealand. His family also lived in Canada when he was a child. Early in his career as an engineer he was an apprentice for the Colonial Sugar Refining Company, later he became a staunch monarchist. Politically he was also anti-communist, and he was a member of the New Guard which was inspired by fascists. I look out of the window again to see the way the airport imposes itself on the land.

Kingsford Smith was also an augur, and he was initiated; he both read signs and created signs for others. His image adorns the old twenty dollar note. He is associated with both capital and this place where I sit waiting, a dominant site of bordering.

Stories continue to travel—uninhibited, they move as a kind of debordering practice. Narrative identity seems more powerful than the subjectivity of my memories, waiting here emphasises this idea. Borderlands are sites of memories, and sometimes the memories of others become part of one's own subjectivity through storytelling practices. I remember once hearing a tale about another prominent site of travel—maybe I heard it when I was a child, maybe sometime after. I am not clear. Two Iranian children used to sit in the *Meidan-e Naqsh-e Jahan* in Isfahan and watch buses pass through. The bulky 1940s buses would enter the almost ninety square-meter public square, emerging from an arch and engulfed by a panorama of elaborately decorated late-medieval structures and surrounded by a ring of arcades—the bazaar. The buses were ushered around the square by the central fountain, lawns and the bustle. The site is characterised by boundaries, but these limits are designed for visual pleasure and to encourage a vibrant and free social life. The Meidan is also a dominant site for visitors and travellers. *Meidan-e Naqsh-e Jahan*, meaning 'image of the world'. Apparently, the two kids would frequent the location regularly to watch the buses pass. Then in the 1950s through to the 1970s they would travel frequently between Iran and Europe for study and work. They would bring carpets to Europe and cars back to Iran. The signs were different then, but clearly those children who became men were also augers.

I move to a café near the departure gate for an espresso—a double. The place is not full, but an eclectic group are scattered throughout. I sit down to drink and a WhatsApp text appears from Manus Island. It is the text I had been waiting for. It is Behrouz, another message to translate for Twitter. Behrouz Boochani is one of my friends from Manus—he has been imprisoned there six years now. The contrast between our journeys is surreal; while I had guides to show me how to read the signs and become initiated, he was left to the violent whim of borders, unlike Kingsford Smith who both exploited his role as auger and produced new signs for control and exclusion.

But Behrouz is initiated in other ways and he is privy to other configurations of signs and ways of reading. The contrasts between us ignite an uncanny logic based on two divergent experiences of displacement and exile: he is Kurdish, from Ilam Province and is the product of generations of resistance against power; was born after the Iranian Revolution, had a rural upbringing and was educated while a religious dictatorship was in power, forced to flee as an adult (for political reasons related to his journalism and cultural advocacy) and tried to seek asylum in Australia by boat. I have Persian ethnicity and come from a family that have experienced various forms of persecution, born before the Iranian Revolution and left Iran as a child during that period (for political and religious reasons), first for the US where we did not manage to gain a Green Card and then Australia where I lived most of my life before years of travelling around the world as an adult. Collaboration with him has allowed us to benefit from each other's insights, a form of border crossing, a debordering practice facilitated by WhatsApp and a zeal for resistance. Our greatest achievement in this respect is the creation of the English book translation of *No Friend but the Mountains: Writing from Manus Prison* (Picador: 2018). Behrouz Boochani's articles and social media announcements are pivotal documents about how people's lives have been reduced to a perverse and brutal form of waiting. We draw on each other's experiences and together develop a creative and theoretical form of resistance we call Manus Prison theory. We are in vastly different circumstances, but we read signs together, we work together, we resist together, we wait together. I visited him three times, but on my fourth attempt I was deported from Papua New Guinea for no legitimate reason—the power of my passport did not work in my favour on this occasion.

I open the new message. Another attempted suicide. It is just weeks after the election and the incarcerated refugees are desperate and feel hopeless. Scott Morrison was Immigration Minister when they were first exiled, and now he is the Prime Minister. The messages cross many borders to communicate what takes place in that borderland. In this case the first location the message arrives is a departure gate at Kingsford Smith. Another point of contrast between us: I cross borders at will, he is forced to wait in an Australian constructed borderland—what he calls Manus Prison.

I am still tweaking the tweet and passengers are boarding. Another sign. Before I received the message, I was eagerly waiting to depart, now I am hoping for some more time. These signs are not only hard to read but are paradoxical. Coffee is cold. Anxious to complete the task. I rush over to board, check for my passport one more time, show it with my boarding pass and move through. But I only encounter another long queue outside the door to the plane. Waiting once again.

The paradoxical performance is almost complete, signs of arrival have passed, signs of departure are emerging. Departing dictates an exceptional kind of order; like arriving, it is thwarted by waiting.

Refugees Welcome?

Hayfaa Chalabi

In *Refugees Welcome?*, Hayfaa Chalabi writes and draws about what kind of design the Migration Board uses to visualise the asylum process. She tells about her own asylum experience and the roles that refugees are forced into. The work becomes a place for memory and history writing where Chalabi tries to understand how to document a process that is prohibited to be documented by the person undergoing it. Illustration in Chalabi's work is a tool that serves an aim beyond its practical aspect of depicting a narrative. It is a resistance against the restrictions of filming, recording, and photographing whatever happens inside the Migration Board's offices in Sweden.

The following illustrations (pp. 98-103) are excerpts from the graphic novel "Refugees Welcome?" by Hayfaa Chalabi, an ongoing project which began as a masters thesis project while studying Visual Communication at Konstfack, University for Arts, Crafts and Design in Stockholm.

Asymmetries

Alessandro Petti, Sandi Hilal and Salvatore Porcaro

The Road Map

The territories of Israel and Palestine are a laboratory. It is a region where, within just a few acres, an incredible variety of borders, enclosures, fences, checkpoints, and controlled corridors are concentrated. In January 2003, we tried to measure, with EU passports, the density of border devices in the surrounding areas of Jerusalem. Along with a person with an Israeli passport, we travelled on Highway 60 from the Israeli colony of Kiriat Arba to the colony of Kudmin. Then, with a person with a Palestinian passport, we travelled from the city of Hebron to the city of Nablus. The two routes both start and end in the same latitude; at some points they overlap. Their travelling times, though, are profoundly different. The difference in temporality is due to the fact that Israeli travellers can use highways—often in tunnels or elevated—which link colonies and bypass Palestinian villages. Palestinian travellers, on the other hand, must cross a number of both permanent and temporary checkpoints—or try to avoid them altogether.

From A to B

In January 2003 we conducted a field study, the results of which reveal the effects of the regime of 'sterile roads,' Israeli military jargon for roads that have been decontaminated of Palestinians. We conducted the following experiment on two different days. The first day we travelled along the route taken by an Israeli colonist to go from the Kiriat Arba colony to the Kedumim colony. The next day we travelled along the route taken by a Palestinian to reach the city of Nablus, starting from Hebron. Both trips start and finish at the same latitude.

The first trip, in an Israeli taxi, took one hour and five minutes; the second, using various Palestinian group taxis, took five hours and twenty minutes. The difference in the journey times was due to several factors: along the route taken by the Palestinian traveller, we had to pass through a number of checkpoints, cover some distance on foot, and change taxi; whereas for the route the Israeli traveller took, we used the bypass roads and passed through the checkpoints without being stopped.

> **From Hebron to Nablus** | January 13, 2003
> Distance: 60 miles
> Duration: 5 hours 20 minutes.

January 13, 2003. We leave from the historical centre of Hebron in the H1 special zone, where Palestinians are under semi-permanent curfew. On foot, we head toward the first checkpoint separating the historical centre from the rest of the city. We take a group taxi which drives us as far as the limits of Area B. The road is blocked by a barrier built by Israel to stop vehicles with white Palestinian license plates from entering Bypass Road 60. We get out of the taxi and pass through the barrier on foot. On the other side, we find a bus reserved for Palestinians that goes as far as Bethlehem. During the trip, the bus stops to pick up other passengers. There are no cars with white Palestinian number plates on this part of the road; the bus is the only vehicle allowed to travel along the bypass road from Hebron to Bethlehem.

We stop in front of a checkpoint at the gates of Bethlehem. Israeli soldiers search the bus. Shortly afterwards, we get off the bus and pass through the checkpoint on foot. On the other side, we find another group taxi which we use to continue our trip. We cannot proceed north using Bypass Road 60, which bypasses Bethlehem going toward Jerusalem, because it is forbidden to Palestinians who do not have a special entry permit. We are forced to detour toward the south-west. At Beit Sahour, we change taxis again. We go down a secondary street that is particularly dangerous, with lots of checkpoints. Whether we'll be able to take this route or not is uncertain. We come across various Israeli army jeeps that are patrolling the roads. The taxi drivers call each other on their phones to exchange information on which roads are passable and free of military patrols. Taking various winding roads, we get to Al 'Ubeidiya. The taxi driver asks us to get out because there's a mobile checkpoint up ahead that he can't go around with the car. Following the other passengers, we go around it on foot and further on, 150 meters in the distance, we find other taxi drivers who are waiting to take us to the next checkpoint.

We reach Abu Dis. The taxi stops next to huge reinforced concrete retaining blocks that divide Abu Dis from East Jerusalem. Here we find other taxis that continue on toward the north. They confirm that we can get at least as far as Ramallah. But they don't know if we can get any further than that. They tell us that once we get to Ramallah we'll find out if there are any taxis for Nablus. During the trip, we leave Area B near Ma'ale Admim, taking Road 1 until it intersects with Road 458. Here, we see a lot of cars with yellow Israeli license plates and group taxis with white Palestinian plates. We get to the Qalandiya checkpoint between Jerusalem and Ramallah. At the checkpoint, we find a taxi for Nablus. We go back along a section of the road to be able to hook up with Bypass Road 60 going north. We are surrounded by a large number of colonist cars.

We continue our trip without stopping. Various colonies come into view as we drive past them. When the road narrows and becomes unpaved, there are no more colonies to be seen. Long before reaching Nablus, the taxi abandons the main road to take a secondary street running through an olive orchard. We ask the taxi driver why he doesn't continue along the road that leads directly to Nablus. He answers that further on there's a checkpoint that we can't get through. We go on through the olive trees until we come out again onto the bypass road. We drive along it for a short distance until coming to the Nablus entry checkpoint. We cross it on foot, showing our European passports to the soldiers, who are very surprised to find us there. Many of the Palestinians are forced to go back.

Once we have crossed the checkpoint, we take a new taxi which drives us to Nablus. The taxi drivers in Nablus tell us that we can't continue north because there are no passable roads. The army has closed all the roads today, they say. But after waiting for a few minutes, one taxi driver claims that he knows which roads to take to get around the checkpoint. We get into his taxi and take a dirt road, through the middle of the countryside, until the taxi driver tells us to get out before a checkpoint that will lead us back onto a normal road. In the distance, soldiers shout at us with rifles pointed that no one is allowed through here. Our journey ends here.

From Kiriat Arba to Kedumim | January 14, 2003
Distance: 60 miles
Duration: 1 hour 5 minutes

January 14, 2003. From the colony of Kiriat Arba, with a yellow-plated Israeli taxi, we start off on Bypass Road 60. We pass through the first checkpoint we come to without stopping. We note that some of the sections of the road we're on are the same ones we travelled along in the Palestinian bus. There are no cars with white Palestinian license plates. We pass through the checkpoint before arriving at the entry to Jerusalem. We bypass Bethlehem through a tunnel and viaduct. At some points, the road is protected from stone-throwing by barriers. The bypass road climbs over the Palestinian village of Beit Jalla, passing above it like a bridge. We drive through the traffic for Jerusalem, continuing northwards. At the checkpoint, we are stopped. After a few questions, we are allowed to continue. We proceed to the colony of Kedumim, where our journey finishes.

This text is an excerpt from Alessandro Petti and Sandi Hilal's recent book "Permanent Temporariness" (Stockholm: Art and Theory Publishing, 2019). The following images (pp. 110-111) were part of the installation "The Road Map" by Multiplicity, 2003. Images courtesy and © the artist.

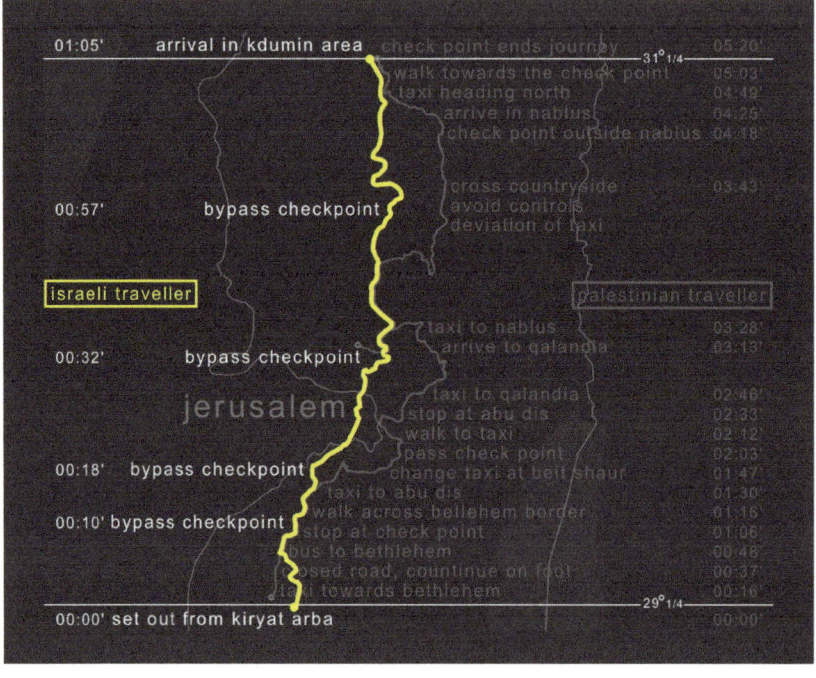

Asymmetries

01:05'	arrival in kdumin area	check point ends journey 05:20'
		walk towards the check point 05:03'
		taxi heading north 04:49'
		arrive in nablus 04:25'
		check point outside nablus 04:18'
		cross countryside 03:43'
00:57'	bypass checkpoint	avoid controls
		deviation of taxi
israeli traveller		**palestinian traveller**
		taxi to nablus 03:28'
00:32'	bypass checkpoint	arrive to qalandia 03:13'
	jerusalem	taxi to qalandia 02:46'
		stop at abu dis 02:33'
		walk to taxi 02:12'
00:18'	bypass checkpoint	pass check point 02:03'
		change taxi at beit shaur 01:47'
		taxi to abu dis 01:30'
00:10'	bypass checkpoint	walk across betlehem border 01:16'
		stop at check point 01:06'
		bus to bethlehem 00:48'
		closed road, countinue on foot 00:37'
		taxi towards bethlehem 00:16'
00:00'		set out from hebron 00:00'

Waiting among Dead Trees

Shahram Khosravi

It is early afternoon. A late Summer day. A small village in the Bakhtiari region along the Zagros mountains in southwestern Iran. Darab and I sit against the short mud wall of a walnut tree garden and chat. He is in his late sixties and has worked all his life on his own small plot of land. Not getting enough from his land, he also worked as a well digger. His chapped palms, the cracked skin on his hands, resembling the deep cracks in the dried soil under our feet, divulge life-long labouring.

> It gets worse every year. Before, I watered this garden myself. I did flood irrigating. Watered all the trees for hours. I let the water go deep, to reach the roots. Nowadays we only pour some water around the trees. It does not reach down to the roots. These trees have not been watered in a long time. It is just a miracle that they have not dried up yet.

In fact, almost all the trees in the garden are dried up and barren but I say nothing. The sadness in his voice and eyes is already overwhelming.

> Before, I dug three days to reach water. Only by myself. With a shovel and a pick. Today they dig wells with machines, going down hundreds of meters. Maybe more, who knows. For nothing. There is no water anywhere.

That Summer day, outside the once walnut tree garden, I avoid looking into Darab's eyes. I say nothing. I have nothing to say. I think about his suffering, watching the trees die, and the wells drying up, seeing how drought has pushed his sons and daughters into migrant work far away from home. The imposed international sanctions against the country has had devastating consequences on the labour market. Jobs are becoming more and more scarce and Darab's children have to move further and further away in search of a job.

I imagine him digging deep, searching for water. Deep in the earth, it is dark and silent. Every now and then he would pause and push his ears to the sidewalls and listen carefully, hoping to hear water. Since he was a kid, he has been digging in the earth to make a livelihood, searching for a fortune he could not find on the surface of the earth. And now he is witnessing that all fade away; rain, water, trees, sons, daughters.

> It rains stones from the sky.

We sit leaning against the mud wall of a fomer walnut garden. We are both looking at the mountains in the distance in silence. The sky is blue with not a cloud in sight. Pointing at the dried, barren, but still standing walnut trees, Darab says

> I do not let people cut them down. They are still beautiful.

Ecologies of Waiting: Stories of a Vacant Land

Sepideh Karami

Lurking sleepiness

The observer is awake. Insomnia makes him *wait* a long time for the first signs of sleepiness. A constant waiting for something unexpected. An anxiety about missing or having missed the first moment of that unexpected event that could finally spark the first line of the story: the story of the vacant land. A siren is heard from afar. Besides the occasional roar of a car passing down the street on the left side of the block, the night is relatively silent. The struggle is between keeping the windows open and suffering a blocked nose due to the pollution hanging over the city or keeping them closed and tossing about on the sofa. The struggle soon resolves in keeping the windows open; the city air rushes in, bringing the hissing sound of night and the aura of unseen crimes. Even in the dark, the vacant land opposite is clearly visible from the top floor flat, where the observer is leaning against the window's handrail and is imagining the ongoing stories behind the weakly lit windows of the buildings opposite; the stories that are lurking behind the semi-closed shades and strengthened by the dim figures passing by the gaps. He moves his eyes from east to west, randomly pausing on the lower and upper windows of the residential buildings lining the edge of the opposite block. After his voyage amongst the imagined lives of others behind the lit and unlit windows, he lowers his gaze to the vacant land lying in between two five-storey buildings: a university building on the left and a residential building on the right. The vacant land is separated from the yard belonging to his building by a white stone wall. It then stretches up to a brick wall with a dark red rusty door on its left corner that opens on to the land on the next street. A single short tree stands off the centre of the land towards the south; the rest seems empty.

The observer doesn't know how long the vacant land has been vacant, although he remembers the land from his childhood, when it was one of three empty plots in a row opposite their balcony; the other two now have buildings on them. He also remembers when the vacant land was the escape route for the burglar, who, one spring night, escaped from the yard and disappeared into the darkness. Other than those rare occasions, the land has been there without that much to say. The observer though hears the murmuring voice of the land telling its stories through gestures only readable to a real observer with acute attention and keen eyes: the single tree, the irregularly grown grasses, the overturned bucket, the tiny little chicken coops here and there, sacks of some sort of soft material, empty aluminium cans of cooking oil with the image of a swan encircled in a blue background, piles of chopped vegetables and watermelon rinds, the occasional stealthy visits by a man, and the earth itself holding all these together: an archive of stories of a vacant land.

Thinking of the earth takes the observer back to the old days, when the land was not a rectangular piece of land but continuous terrain expanding over a village called Mobarak Abad located beyond the gates of old Tehran; the name refers to what the village was famous for: green, flourishing, fertile lands. The observer imagines the fig and pomegranate trees spreading their branches under the sunshine, sparrows flying on the breeze over the cultivated fields and lush gardens. He imagines farmers leaving the fields at sunset with sun-tanned faces and deep lines around their eyes, chickens here and there scratching the dirt tracks, pecking invisible morsels, the scent of freshly baked bread drifting on the air. He hears the sound of streams originating from the subterranean well that runs through the roots of the fig trees, pomegranate trees and fields of vegetables and legumes that turn the village into scenic greenery. The image belongs to the 19th century, during which this scenic greenery and the charming weather of the village, with its 258 inhabitants,[1] turned it into a destination for Naser al-Din Shah, one of the Kings of the Qajar dynasty, and his allies; a favourite verdurous place for royal banquets. The observer imagines the cool summer breeze blowing over the huge moustache of Naser-al-Din Shah as he observes the village from the windows of his coach, proud of *owning* a country.

The King's excursion

On the 3rd of October 1892, a sunny autumn day, the observer pauses on a ladder by a fig tree, turns his head to the sound of galloping horses pulling a blue coach with golden ornaments along the dirt track passing by the fields; a crowd of villagers are cheering for the King while disappearing in the cloud of dust behind the coach and its army of escorting horses.[2] The observer spots the King's huge moustache behind his dusty coach windows and realises it is another of Naser al-Din Shah's excursions to Mobarak Abad. That day, the King has been invited to the village by Mirza Abdullah Khan Yooshi, whose two sisters will become his wives. The observer, standing on the ladder, thinks about the banquet prepared for the King and wonders how many of his garden's figs were used in the recipes. He drops a ripe fig on the ground and says in despair: one for the land.

Four years later, on the 31st of April 1896, when the observer hears of the King being assassinated, he is again up on the ladder, checking the fig trees. While he remembers the fig that he dropped four years ago

---

1 Hossein Karimian, *Qasran* (Tehran: Anjoman-e-Asar-e-Melli, 1977), 533.
2 Mohsen Moetamedi, *Joghrafiay e Tarikhi e Tehran* (Tehran: Nashr-e-Danieshgahi, 2002), 393.

from top of the ladder and how it became part of the soil, part of the roots, part of the trees, he thinks of the King's moustache: "if he doesn't survive the bullet, his decomposing body soon becomes part of the soil, part of the trees, part of the land," and whispers: "one for the land."

The day after, on the first of May a child is running on along the dirt tracks of the village of Mobarak Abad, shouting: "THE KING IS DEAD...", cackling chickens running away. The observer is washing his hands in the narrow stream running past the garden of fig trees and choked by the dust raised by the child running, who by now is being followed by around ten more kids, leisurely announcing the death of the King. The observer coughs and thinks of Naser al-Din Shah's moustache once more and wonders what it is in the chemical structure of the hair that doesn't become part of the earth even after years of decomposition. Forty days later, when the figs are ripe, the observer hears of the coronation of the new King, Mozaffar al-Din Shah, the 43-year-old prince.

After that event, the village and its lands changed hands several times. Despite his father, the new king never came to the village, but the ownership of the village was handed over to his Prime Minister, Abdol Majid Mirza Eyn-ed-Dowleh, who built himself a mansion and a garden there. In 1911, when the village gradually lost its prosperity and scenic greenery, men of wealth and power stopped visiting the village and instead it gradually became part of urban and real estate development. Ten years later, when Reza Heravi purchased the land from Eyn-ed-Dowleh and developed cultural and educational infrastructures, the area thrived once more.[3] But the force of urbanisation along with political shifts of power, revolutions and so on, created new urban characters as land speculators, whose numbers increased with the ticking of time. These new urban characters amputated the farmlands from the rest of the terrain. Farmlands became fragmented rec-

---

3 Soudabeh Ranjbar, "Heravi: Khatereh Mandegar e Mobarak Abad," in *Hamshahri Online*, 2018, accessed October 20, 2019, http://newspaper.hamshahrionline.ir/id/10600

tangular pieces of land waiting to become buildings. Others remained empty as a source of progressive accumulated wealth created by the increasing housing problems for unprivileged urban dwellers and rural immigrants to the big cities.

Mr. Mayor and amputated terrain

The vacant land, amputated from the rest of its body by a history of ownership, occupation, land reform and urbanisation, is among more and more rarely found vacant plots in the densely constructed city of Tehran. These vacant plots left in between high-rises and carelessly built buildings, preserved from inept developers, have become the plots of formal and informal urban acts in a state of waiting. Many of these lands have remained vacant for years, some owned by those who fled the country in the aftermath of the 1979 revolution. In the power vacuum following the revolution and the absence of owners, some were taken over by squatters, and later on by the Mostazafan Foundation of the Islamic Revolution with the intention of expropriation under the name of handing them over to the public poor.

Mr. Mayor has followed many of these lands since the 1979 Iranian Revolution. The observer has seen Mr. Mayor twice, from his top floor flat's window wandering around the opposite vacant land. Mr. Mayor, though, has never become a mayor, but has been waiting to become one. While waiting for the right moment to step in and put himself up for mayoral election, he works as a janitor of a residential building, writing and working hard on his *theories* of urban vacant lands. When the revolution happened, and one of its slogans was to give power to the poor, he was excited by the very thought of the possibility of becoming a mayor. But those in positions of decision-making asked him to wait a bit longer for things to be stabilised, so that the enemies of the Revolution couldn't destroy what had been achieved. He waited, and while waiting read many books, talked to many people, visited many vacant lands, hopped on many busses, waited under many bridges, watched many movies, imagined himself in many cities: London with red busses, Paris with street cafés, Delhi with many motorcycles, Venice with many boats.

He reviewed Urban Wasteland Ownership Abolition Law and took notes in his series of black notebooks about the two terms in Iranian Islamic land law appointed to vacant urban land: *mavat* and *bayer*. *Mavat* is "land that is undeveloped and that has no prior record of development" and *bayer* is "land that previously had been developed but that had fallen into disuse."[4] He knew that this classification created different ownership status under the law over time. For example, the 1979 Urban Wasteland Ownership Abolition Law, that was approved six months after the revolution, brought some tension to the private ownership of urban wastelands.[5] According to this law, based on the detailed city plan, the government had to tell the private owners of the vacant lands to initiate the development in a given time frame. If the owners did not show up, the government would take hold of the land. This created some complicated situations as many of the private owners had fled the country and couldn't return for political reasons. As a result, solicitors and lawyers became busier than ever, running up and down the courts, making international calls discussing deeds with their clients. Mr. Mayor has observed these scenes as well.

Later, when the end of the war between Iran and Iraq in 1988 brought relative stability, some of the owners with legal deeds could claim their land back. Mr. Mayor has seen many children of the owners visiting the land. For example, he remembers one who travelled from England and was unhappy with the florist who had occupied their land, built a water well in the middle of it and had turned the land into a garden. Mr. Mayor also saw two siblings who travelled from San

---

4 A.-Ch Kiss and Johan G. Lammers, *Hague Yearbook of International Law: Vol. 10: 199*, (Leiden: Brill., 1997), 212.

5 Mohammad Mehdi Azizi, "Evaluation of Urban Land Supply Policy in Iran." in *International Journal of Urban and Regional Research* 22/1 (2002): 96.

Diego and were happy that the brick wall enclosing their land was still there, almost untouched. While Mr. Mayor was watching the siblings from across the street, the observer saw him from the window of his top floor flat for the first time.

Mr. Mayor and his theory of subtle occupation

Many solicitors and their clients won their cases in court and could reclaim their pieces of land. But many of those lands remained undeveloped, fenced off and marked "No Entry. This Is a Private Property." Mr. Mayor, though, has developed his own theory about these lands and suggests they produce their own ecologies over years of waiting. Mr. Mayor thinks of the stories accumulated in these lands, in the earth and in the remaining infrastructures during the period of waiting. He thinks of these lands as silent archives; having waited long under rain, thick snow, decomposing leaves, urinating passers-by, the excrement of crows and cats, dead mosquitos, flies and bees, and perhaps a hair from the moustache of Naser al-Din Shah. All buried, layers on layers, years after years waiting for their stories to be told. Such plots are no longer urban surfaces to be occupied but are *thickened* through years of *waiting* while hosting events and stories. He believes telling these stories can gather together all living and non-living human and non-human characters that once inhabited these vacant lands and can enrich the earth.

Mr. Mayor thinks these stories should be actively continued. To speculate over how these stories can be continued he has written pages and pages on his theory of *subtle occupation* i.e. *growing an urban ecology in suspended ownership*. Contrary to overt occupation that changes the existing relations of the plot and exposes the act of occupation, subtle occupation, he argues, can happen through minimum intervention in the site that renders the ongoing act of occupation invisible. In other words, the land seems empty, while activities go on covertly without the owner noticing, and importantly, without any violation of the initial ownership. Mr. Mayor not only writes these theories, but also conducts experiments. And this morning he is proudly thinking of his own experiment in subtle occupation, an aviculture in nearby vacant land that has lasted for years without being stopped by the state or the owners, the two siblings from San Diego. He looks out at the pink dawn and thinks that his night shift will be over soon and he can drop by *his* land before city life starts, to feed his chickens and take care of the subtle infrastructures he has set up on the site.

The fox

Foxes know how to approach human habitats at night, intrude through small holes and gaps to find food and vanish before being caught. It's why they have survived in Tehran without often being observed. Like many other nights, while the observer is looking out of the window, foxes are possibly doing their mischief somewhere in the city. The observer, though, is not thinking about foxes but about how out-of-control urbanisation has taken over fields and rural areas. And it is just when he is thinking about the escalating value of land coupled with a sense of nostalgia for farmland in the historical images of this area of Tehran, he becomes distracted by a furry thing moving in the vacant land. At second glance, he spots a fox. The fox is friskily taking the chickens by their necks out of their coops and leaving them in the middle of the plot. Now the night is ornamented by the chickens' cackles. The observer waits for the fox to be done with his wild adventure. When he thinks the fox is done, he hisses very slowly, but the fox spots him behind the window on the top floor. The fox hesitates for two seconds and then runs away from the hole beside the metal door. The plot resembles a massacre against the newly born dawn.

An hour later, when the observer can hardly keep his eyes open, finally what he has been waiting for happens. Mr. Mayor descends the small steps that he has made himself by the metal door. He steps on the ground and freezes in shock: his chickens, here and there, dead or semi-alive; blood splashed on the ground. Only three of them, still alive, walking around, scratching the earth, pecking at food, and the observer writes:

> A crow on the slim branches of the long tree in the neighbouring land, weighs itself against the pink-greyish sky. Up and down in a leisurely manner, it dives down to where the three chickens have gathered, reaches the land, picks something up quickly, flies back up to the sky, and perches on the edge of the next building. Up there, the crow flips its wings in a display of victory and clicks its beak to re-taste the food. Mr. Mayor doesn't move, and the crow's caw pierces the early morning sky.

Thanks to Babak Karami for thinking with me while I was writing the stories of the vacant land.

Ecologies of Waiting: Stories of a Vacant Land 127

An empty plot in the Tehran grid. Photograph by Sepideh Karami, 2019.

after the blast: near silence, rising

mirko nikolić

A trench, a hole in the ground,
one can walk into it and disappear from sight
in the forest, stones
and plants and animals scarred, a community
of beings expelled,
gold-chasers, silver-hunters, nickel-entrepreneurs have arrived
scrambling for the riches of the earth
to 'cut and run,' enclose and export
fortunes for free, almost, all but

It started in the nineteen-sixties,
with experts picking with tiny hammers
then, as the results got more interesting,
bulldozers, test-drills, dynamite sticks were called in
a water well was contaminated, a small price for the explorers
bodies were duly marked, classified,
a few more commodity cycles after
when the Finnish nation-state aligned better with the global market
and the invitation reached the extraction empires
a London-based company controls the fates of these rocks
they dream of 'innovating' money

There is law, and then there is calculus
this trench right here was torn open whilst waiting for
the permission to mine, from very permissive authorities
some blast the queue, if they can pay to
the hole asks for more drills, authorities are to blame too slow,
for extractivists' taste, so they decide
let's cut short checks and consultations
two-hundred-and-twenty tonnes of earth are snuck out
to test, to squeeze ounces of gold, while
back in the forest, arsenic might yet seep
into the nearby brook, travel across
the membranes and bloodstreams
undoing life

In the capital of metal exchange
this self-proclaimed lion waves colourful maps and spreadsheets
to attract investors, but his fortunes are yet to prosper
sometimes a vague dread fills him,
has he done everything 'right'? he well knows
there are only degrees of doing it not exactly right
an extractivist's time is precious, filled with hustling
there is no time to walk into the woods
to feel the rain, he detests waiting
profitable time lost

After all, the nation-state cries that it wants more holes,
more jobs, more metal, more stuff,
so he knows, sort of, that it will be 'alright'
they are both on the same side by origin, history, project
the state can hardly resist rejoining the capital,
redeploying its powers once more
in primitive accumulation, war by other names
relocating bodies of the suburbs, the backwoods, the borders
to clear cut frictions

When extractivists manage to outwait the state
he might yet succeed in tearing open new holes,
but small companies need to rush
the big ones can afford the wait,
invest effort in wearing down the authorities, the locals
through courts, appeals, resubmissions,
if the application is turned down, he might even sue the sluggish state
try to pocket some cash claiming hypothetical losses
some get paid for waiting
and some need not wait while everyone else must,
extraction commands time in these lands
it is essential, it should never stop
before all, the state came after copper, gold, iron

But it's not only these powers
that speak, that discuss, agree
in the vacuum of board rooms,
once he cuts into the mesh of the earth
a billion frictions, unplanned, spring up
everywhere dwell monsters, who seem hellbent on slowing down
the march of over- and its twin under- development,
undercurrents sit or stand or lie in the road
in the trees in the ground
there are other dreams, other paces
many labours and worlds

That spot on the map, stripped by the explosion,
it is no tabula rasa,
has never been empty
it has a name, many names,
a forest, a village, a community
who have been silenced, gradually, through austerities and abandonment
the shop shut, the post gone, the school closed,
jobs first given then taken back to the city,

even in this overdeveloped country
the smooth flow of progress meanders
a good life is not given once and to all,
globalised supply and imperial demand lurk to jump in
to fill the gaps left by democracy, rights, freedoms

Silencing does not equal silence
the inhabitants retell histories of dispossession and debt
of not that long ago, while some
expect someone or something to 'save' this
beautiful village next to a beautiful lake
revive memories of music and dancing together,
what's shaping however is a conversion into an export zone,
a bleak drive-in treasury, while authorities pretend
that mutually exclusive stories are compossible,
one day it's clear that they know only binaries:
jobs or waters, fish or gold, smoke or air,
either or's
a hegemonic imperative
policed and enforced
because it is deeply untrue

Decision-makers, extractivists, explorers,
perhaps they do not know this blot on the map
has always been, will always be brimming with
dwellers, neighbours,
in dozens, in thousands of shapes, skins, voices,
who face the capital as its messengers trot in
unexpected and uninvited
the forest-dwellers remember the previous fortune-sellers
watch closely, discern full well who cares
from who cuts corners, who sows hope and promises of
prosperity, while thinking plunder
shock and awe

toxicity radiates before and after imperial cold
tools and weapons

In the forest, around the blasted ground
silence never sits still, it wells up
bodily memory and learning
waters, animals, symbionts thread new paths
the forest is gathering, reorganising around its scars,
is there anger at injustice, in this rising so smooth yet tenuous
or patience and resistance
trust in coexistence

And the village is organising
reconnecting with others,
learning biochemistry, geology, technology
transnational protocols and laws of the state
unpaid labours incomparable to the wages that extractivists pay
to pressure, to push, to break
the tissues of community
to then crack those of the earth
it is not possible to compare
capitalist and
reproductive labours
incommensurable worlds of value

It has been two years, it has been seven, fourteen
of applications, negotiations,
the community heard promises, tricks and threats
uncertainty piled up in the bones, sleepless nights, exhausted
relationships, while the decision is being conspired elsewhere
or just left to sit on a shelf
abandoned, while the interests secretly moved on
leaving behind a mosaic of tiny little divides,
rumours, confusion

awkward silences among those you thought you knew,
some of you become a minority at home
struggling to liberate time captivated
by the extraction empire, to shake off
its acid persuasions, to clean up
its dust and debris

You she ze I we are not alone in this
allies, close and far, known and not-yet-known, listen
even when no one seems to be coming, many are
alongside, underneath, just above, calling
in the canopies, in the soil
passages, mangles, commons
migrations, respirations, pollinations
the living and the nonliving
we remember and reinvent, nearness
transgressions of boundaries
in near silence, dense with yearning
you have been expecting us, in long
herstories of resistance

Photograph by mirko nikolić, 2020.

Standing in Line

Shahram Khosravi

One paradigmatic image of societies which struggle with poverty and undemocratic governance is the queue. Long and slow-moving queues outside official buildings, stores where subsidised goods are offered, job centres, and the embassies of rich countries. Some of them have become permanent. People sleep overnight in queues to be at the front of the line in the morning. The queuing system has generated its own economy. Vendors are around to sell food and beverages. Brokers offer various real and fake services. Others stand in the queue to keep your place in exchange for money.

People's lives are organised by and with queues. Standing in long, slow-moving, tedious queues has become part of daily life. Generations grow up seeing adults around them spending a large part of their free time in queues for various necessities: food, petroleum, clothing, or other household items. People conceptualise life through the logic of queues. When seeing a queue, one joins it and then asks what it is for. A queue indicates that something worthy of waiting for is for sale. In many societies ruled under totalitarianism we can see outbreaks of epidemics of queuing. This is best shown by the Kenyan writer Ngũgĩ wa Thiong'o who, in his well-known novel *Wizard of the Crow*[1] tells us how institutionalised corruption and a totalitarian regime sparks off what he calls "queuing mania."

---

1 Ngũgĩ wa Thiong'o, *Wizard of the Crow* (London: Harvill Secker, 2006).

Vladimir Sorokin's novel *The Queue*,² published in English in 1988 depicts how standing in queues had become a fundamental part of daily life in the Soviet Union and how queues had become one of the main elements in forming people's subjectivity. This is also a central theme in *Queues*,³ a work of fiction written by Zimbabwean author Shimmer Chinodya in 2003, who illustrates how life in post-independence Zimbabwe is arranged with and by queues.

In societies ruled by undemocratic states, rather than a lack of resources, queues are often a matter of entitlement to the resources; who has the right to get access to subsidised items and rations and who does not. Citizens who stand for long hours in various queues perform their request for the entitlement, showing their deservingness. The longer you wait, the more your deservingness is shown.

The queues also manifest the state's sovereignty and people's dependence on the state. While access to subsidies is linked to citizenship, waiting for rations and subsidised goods becomes a performance of citizenship. Patiently waiting in queues, waiters *for* the state, citizen are turned into waiters (in both meanings of the word; attendant and one who waits) *of* the state. In his book about his six years as a prisoner under the Australian immigration detention policy on Manus Island, Behrouz Boochani recurrently writes about queues:

> The queue is a replica of a factory production line. Total discipline. Calculated and precise. The first stage is at the end of the line—a place covered by an awning, a place from which no one can tell where the queue ends. The queue makes a turn behind the rooms occupied by Sri Lankans. After at least half an hour, one arrives at the bend and realises that the queue extends for another thirty meters."⁴

---

2 Vladimir Sorokin, *The Queue*, (New York: Readers International, 1988).
3 Shimmer Chinodya, "Queues" in *Staunton, Irene: Writing Still: New stories from Zimbabwe*, ed. Irene Staunton (Harare: Weaver Press, 2003).
4 Behrouz Boochani *No Friend But the Mountains: Writing from Manus Prison* (Sydney: Pan Macmillan, 2018), 191.

Queues are productive; they produce obedient behaviour. Interestingly, Boochani's use of the term 'behaviour' recalls Hannah Arendt's warning about a system of control which replaces action with behaviour.[5] While the former is defined as spontaneous and is characterised by its ineliminable freedom, the latter is predictable and conforms to social norms. Systematically making people stand in queues facilitates control over bodies both spatially and temporally.

The institutionalised queue system generates corruption. Keeping people waiting is a common tactic used by bureaucratic gatekeepers for extortion. Connections and bribes can move you forward in the line faster and a lack of them can mean you are sent backwards.

The Egyptian journalist and author Basma Abdel Aziz's novel *The Queue*,[6] published in English in 2016, is built upon the metaphor of waiting in queues in a fictive country to illustrate how the whole of life under a dictatorship is turned into a queue, in which citizens wait for orders from "the Gate." Read her excellent essay on queues under dictatorship in this volume.

---

5 Hannah Arendt, *The Human Condition*, (Chicago: University of Chicago Press, 1958).
6 Basma Abdel Aziz, *The Queue* (New York: Melville House, 2016).

Golrokh Nafisi, Queues, 2020. Image courtesy and © the artist

Queues 141

The Distance from Here

Bani Abidi

It used to be that the first line of people outside the embassy would form in the early hours of the morning, when it was still dark and cool. These were the years when people were still permitted to enter without appointments. People from out of town would arrive the night before, setting up some form of bedding on the sidewalk. A few hours later, in the early morning, the residents of the city would start joining the queue and find their own corners to squat in. The more privileged ones would send their chauffeurs as proxies to wait in line on their behalf. Some people sat and dozed, children lay and slept, some just stood awake, waiting. As the sun came out, everyone would stir and stretch, looking around to see the new arrivals that had gathered through the night. As if on cue, the tea seller would appear, clanging his teapot and distributing small glasses of tea. Gradually, customary conversations would start: "Where have you come from? Where are you headed? Why? How long has your son lived there? Have you ever been rejected entry?" A brief exchange would occur that would somehow soothe the collective anxiety of this motley crowd, an assurance that they were all in this together.

    Nowhere was there an official marking that indicated where this informal, outside line should begin, and what should be its limit. The queue just began, and others just followed. The first real entry to the premises would only happen through the tall metal barrier at 9am in the morning, and only fifty people would be allowed to enter. By then the sun would be bright, sticky and hot. The only object that everyone had at hand to cover their face were their visa applications. These were files and folders of varying thicknesses and colours, chunky wads of stapled, pinned, bound documents that each person was required to bring with them. They contained visa applications, two-by-two inch photographs with a blue background, bank statements, salary slips, letters from employers, utility bills, birth, marriage and death certificates, school and university degrees, lease agreements, property ownership documents, police clearances, copies of all previous passports, letters of sponsorship and support from their hosts—life dossiers that had taken months to assemble. When the gate opened, only a small number would actually go in. Most of the people waiting in the queue would be just family members accompanying their sons, daughters, husbands, fathers, wives, uncles and aunts, nieces and nephews. They were not applying for a visa and had to wait outside.

Once the small group had entered the premises, each one had to go through an individual security check. They spilled out their wallets, phones, keys, lipsticks, coins, cigarettes, lighters and chewing gum in plastic trays that slowly moved through x-ray machines. After a full body scan, and the collection of their belongings, they were given tokens. Boldly printed numbers on little pieces of paper, which one could easily rip by folding or fiddling with, as one tended to do with little pieces of paper. And these bits of paper felt flimsier in the heat. The group now had to wait in an outdoor shed. There was not enough seating, which meant that some would have to stand, while others would dart across the shed and secure spots for themselves. The heat was not exactly alleviated by the tiny wall fans, which slowly rotated under the four corners of the asbestos ceiling. But there was shade and it was cooler than being in the sun. And there was an electric water cooler with chilled water, provided at no extra cost. Once seated and assigned an interview, an initial calm would take over the group. But this step of waiting outdoors was to last for hours and anxieties would start rising. Gradually, people would become more familiar and chattier with those sitting next to them. Files would be exchanged, and soon enough everyone would rummage through each other's personal papers, one double-checking for the other if everything was in order. The alarmists scared various people with exclamations of missing information. The practical ones would shrug their shoulders and stick to plan. The optimists would assure everyone that only God could determine what was to happen in any case. But inevitably, over a few hours everyone would get to know each other's lives intimately. Every small group summoned indoors over the public speaker would be observed quietly with hushed whispers of "Good Luck" sounding here and there.

The installed speaker had an automated voice with an accent. It would announce the multiple numbers that were permitted entry at one time. The overly chilled air-conditioned indoor waiting room, with its imported waiting room furniture, lush green plants and marble floors already felt like a threshold to the destined country. And just entering it would feel like an achievement to many. Once seated people found themselves facing two interview windows, in which people would have to speak rather loudly to be heard. This would result in a strange experience of being able to rehearse your interview and anticipate questions, or just feel outright fearful, while sitting and staring at other people being interrogated, very loudly.

Having received the final verdict on the spot, people would return victorious or dejected to their anxious families, who had been waiting outside for the whole day. And the day would finally be over.

This was how it used to be, a ritual of waiting, intimidation and authority that we were comfortably familiar with. But then one day, it all changed, all the embassies moved into one neighbourhood in the city and huddled close to each other fearfully. They surrounded the *Diplomatic Enclave* with high barricades, barbed wire, and little armies of private security guards, and we the natives had to acquaint ourselves with new forms of protocol all over again.

This text is a fictional postscript to the short film "The Distance from Here" by Bani Abidi, 2009. The following images (pp. 146-149) are stills from the film. Images courtesy and © the artist.

Bani Abidi

The Distance from Here 147

Waiting in Queues under Dictatorship

Basma Abdel Aziz

A queue can be a powerful and effectively disgracing tool, used by bureaucratic dictatorships in order to dominate people. An image of queueing I witnessed a while ago still stays with me. A group of extremely poor people, mostly elderly women, were queueing under a burning sun in front of a public office. They were waiting their turn to meet officials to ask them to put their names back on the list for social welfare, so they could get access to the subsidised food stuff. They were queueing because their names had unreasonably been removed from the list without any explanation. After a long wait, they had to convince the authorities that they were really poor, old and miserable, and without their help they would starve.

We all wait. Waiting for something to happen is a common experience. Since ancient times, hunters have waited for their prey, farmers have waited for rain, fishermen have waited for good weather. Waiting has become a naturalised part of daily life. However, in a life under dictatorship waiting becomes an eternal nightmare. Bureaucracy as an apparatus which makes people wait becomes part of the oppressive system.

The authorities design numerous waiting situations in which individuals spend a lot of time without making any achievements. Citizens may wait for hours in front of governmental booths to get their documents signed and stamped. They may wait a whole morning in state-run markets for subsidised goods. They may lose a day or more in queues in order to renew a driving license, national ID, a passport, or just to pay a bill. In the horrible, randomly formed queues, which turn up anytime and anywhere, one is often stuck and fails to move forward. A child may never have the chance to be transferred from a faraway school to another nearby one. A seriously ill woman may wait years to receive life-saving treatment. Everyone must wait for every single and simple task to be done.

Waiting is used by an authoritarian system to keep bodies, which are considered to be a pending source of danger, in queues within limited spaces. Waiting mostly takes place in well-defined areas, where citizens are forced to follow orders. In its physical aspect, 'waiting' represents an exhausting process. Standing in prolonged queues means that citizens waste their energy and are pacified.

However, its psychological impact seems far more harmful. To keep citizens waiting is a method of draining people's souls, to keep them in a state of chronic, low-threshold anxiety. People are effectively trained to wait. When a generalised waiting mood possesses the mind of the nation, it exerts its strong pervasive effect over people; so, no behaviours displaying anger, no protests, no marks of refusal, no signs of disobedience can be detected. A person who waits for most of his or her life will become frozen and emptied of their vitality. Gradually stagnation steals the will, implants hollowness instead. This is what the authorities welcome. Queues produce obedient, easily manipulated citizens.

Waiting as punishment is explicitly used against political opponents, who are exposed to endless pre-trial detention. They are locked between walls, without fair trial. Their families are also kept in queues to visit their imprisoned loved ones. As additional punishment, political prisoners are deprived of the right to visits. However, visitors constantly receive vague official promises, which mean they remain hopeful and wait more. The absence of rules and clear orders leaves the door open, but with a wall behind it.

People who are subjected to endless waiting normally feel humiliated and disgraced. In a queue, one loses her personality, her own privileges, and becomes merely a meaningless number in the queue. An uncanny existence in a relatively tight place, where each one is a copy of the other. A citizen in a queue is easily transformed into a shadow of a citizen. In the waiting queues, each person minimises his or her demands. Queues impel the citizen to request less. Anyone who tries to protest against the endless waiting situation is labelled a traitor. No one is allowed to walk out or to break the rules of queueing.

Waiting might become a lifestyle and slowly but surely people get used to standing in a queue, any queue. They might forget that they can simply refuse to wait. They forget that a life without queues is possible.

Good Queue, Bad Queue

Unlike the idea of lines, chaos is an inseparable aspect of queues. If you are able to take your role easily, and other people respect your place in the queue, and no one tries to jump ahead of you, and it is not too hot so you are not sweating and not about to faint; just thank God that you have been lucky enough to join an ideal queue. Queues usually turn into chaos. People tend to gather in bulky masses and move forward out of line. Boredom is characteristic of queues. The waiting scenes are noisy. People scream and frequently fight with each other, maybe to get ahead of each other or for a more comfortable zone to stay in.

In patriarchal societies a queue branches most of the time into two parallel lines; one line for men and the other for women. The division is claimed to protect women from harassment, but it is not always the case. Sometimes women face hostility from the men's side, who generally feel repressed and direct their frustrations towards the women.

Most waiting areas are designed to intensify the sense of humiliation. Waiting in queues not only consumes people's time and dignity, it might also be risky. For instance, people have lost their lives in bread queues. Bread is abundant, you can buy it from any market, but cheap loaves are monopolised by the state. As many people cannot afford the bread available in private markets, they have to wait outside the stores for the arrival of subsidised bread. Since there is never enough for everyone, people end up fighting with each other to get some.

Queues and Hope

Under dictatorship it is like a game, a *waiting game*—a means to keep people waiting and suffering yet letting them remain hopeful. They shall be kept at the edge of frustration's hole, but never pushed down to the bottom.

The relationship which arises between people who are queueing at one side, and the authorities who control them on the other side should be carefully observed. Is it really a single-player game? It is not. While the authorities pretend to be the only player, the people also perform a main role in the game. Thus, one may ask; why do people keep waiting? Why do they follow an inefficient, broken system? What makes them so attached to repressive authority? Why do they queue and wait, instead of revolting in some way?

Lots of ideas come to my mind when thinking about queues and endless waiting. Like this one: if people completely lose hope, the hostile circle of waiting breaks. At the point of complete despair people would give up, retreat from their commitments, abandon their duties, and put an end to their permanent waiting. The rope which ties them to the dominating authority will be cut. Puppets are then freed, regain their moving capacity, become able to leave the queue, and put an end to the whole game.

The following image is the cover of Basma Abdel Aziz's book "The Queue." Image courtesy of Melville House Publishing.

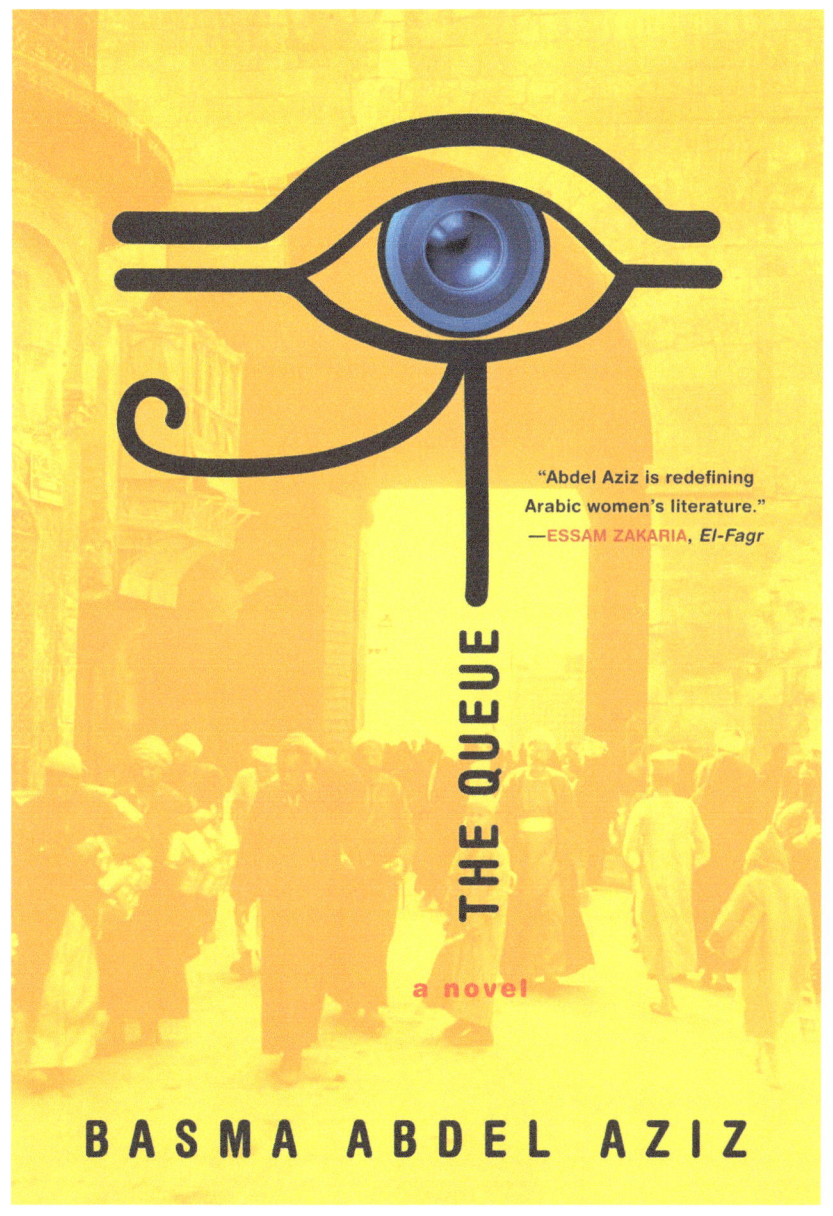

Our Silence will Swell Like a Mountain

Omar Berrada

> You know why there's so much light over there? Because it's dark here. The darker it is here, the lighter over there.[1]

In 2006, Ali Essafi, an accomplished Moroccan filmmaker, watched Ahmed Bouanani's short films *Mémoire 14* (1971) and *6 & 12* (1968) for the first time;

> I felt a flood of emotions—anger but also pride... and some questions I've been asking myself ever since. Why had we, my peers and I, been deprived access to such a major oeuvre? Would I have followed the same path if I had known Bouanani's works when I was 20 years old?[2]

When I finally laid my hands on Bouanani's novella *L'Hôpital*, I had a similar reaction to Essafi, realising I had also been waiting forever for this work. During Morocco's Years of Lead,[3] Bouanani's works were removed from bookstores, libraries, and theatres. He was pushed into muteness.

---

1 *Tarfaya* (2004, 90'), dir. Daoud Aoulad-Syad, screenplay by Youssef Fadel. Miriam, the film's protagonist, utters these words while looking at the city of Fuerteventura in the Canary Islands, from a balcony in Tarfaya, Morocco.
2 Ali Essafi, "La medersa Bouanania li cinéma al maghribia" in *Nejma* #9 (2014). Authors translation.
3 The *Years of Lead* refers to the period between the 1960s and the 1980s during the rule of King Hassan II of Morocco, marked by state violence and oppression of political dissidents.

Censorship kept entire generations cloaked in thick expectant fog, struggling to read the silences, striving to make sense of their own cultural and historical surroundings. How many more voices remain stuck in the purgatories of our cultural infrastructure? Are we meant to wait until they magically emerge from decades of dust? We are haunted by a past we have not known, though we believe it holds the keys to our future. We wait, but we never rest, for "mute memory has no testament."[4]

Breaks in transmission are common in postcolonial societies. They materialise the eternal return of colonial trauma—a wall perpetually erected between our heritage and ourselves. For Frantz Fanon, the breaking of a population's systems of reference is a condition of economic and biological subjugation.[5] As their embrace of neoliberal and neocolonial policies makes clear, the authoritarian regimes of newly 'independent' nations understood this early on. What were we expecting?

In 2001, before he met Bouanani, before he had a chance to watch *Mémoire 14* or *6 & 12*, Essafi made an hour-long documentary titled *Ouarzazate Movie*. "Ouarzazate, a small town in the south of Morocco, ekes out a living from meagre benefits left by international film productions."[6] Ouarzazate hosts some of the largest film studios in the world. Parts of *Lawrence of Arabia*, *The Last Temptation of Christ*, *Gladiator*, *The Mummy* and *Game of Thrones* were shot there. Producers are attracted to the endless available space, the picturesque architecture, the desert scenery, and above all the cheap Labour.

By observing life in and around film sets, *Ouarzazate Movie* examines a predatory industry that relies on countless extras from neighbouring villages and treats them like cattle. In need of income, women and men, young and old, are perpetually waiting for 'the cinema' to

---

4 Ahmed Bouanani, *The Shutters*. Trans. Emma Ramadan (New Directions, 2018).

5 Frantz Fanon, "Racism and culture" in *Toward the African Revolution*, trans. Haakon Chevalier (New York: Grove Press, 1964).

6 Ali Essafi, *Ouarzazate Movie* (2001, 57'), opening screen.

come to town. Once a new production is announced, they all line up to apply for employment. They huddle on the bleachers of a soccer stadium, behind a chain link fence under the blazing sun until a production assistant shows up to pick the lucky ones. Behind the fence, they are nothing but their age, gender, skin tone, or physical type. Their time does not belong to them. They are not applying for a specific role. Their only choice is to wait for hours until they are called, or asked to go home.

In the Ouarzazate studios, waiting is absolute. No explanations are given. No expectations are allowed. The whole process is a well-oiled, if chaotic-looking machine. It upholds the racial-economic border symbolised by the chain link fence. At one point, a villager mentions a director he worked with on 11 films, who never even acknowledged him. At the end of each shoot, however, he would come ask all the extras to clap in recognition of the main (white) actor's performance.

"When I walked through the large iron gate of the hospital, I must have still been alive."[7] Thus opens Ahmed Bouanani's *The Hospital*. It too documents the marginalisation of a specific group of people—tuberculosis patients in 1960s Morocco. The spatial separation between the hospital and the city, between the sick and the healthy, the human and the less than human immediately translates into temporal segregation;

> The nurse leading me to Wing C proudly wore a Swiss watch on his wrist, undoubtedly purchased on the black market. As we walked, he'd announced the time twice to the groups of invalids slumped on the ground or straddling the low walls. I felt that perhaps this was his reason for being. Not only did he shout out the time, but he also took care to specify the seconds —and the thousandths of seconds—to men frozen here for days or weeks and who seemed to harbour all the necessary indifference to the passage of time and changes in the calendar. Was it his way of distancing himself from this ailing humanity?[8]

---

7 Ahmed Bouanani, *The Hospital*, trans. Lara Vergnaud (New Directions, 2018), 37.
8 Ibid.

One patient explains that, despite living in the hospital for years, he;

> Can't count the days because their deceptive number has in fact been reduced to a single day that lasts 'inside' of each of us, and that day is a single point that can contain the entire universe, infinity.[9]

The patients live in the stasis of a sort of existential waiting. Time has thickened beyond duration. Some of them are not waiting anymore. Frail health can hardly withstand such massive abandonment. Death is their daily companion. The institution of care is really an infrastructure of coercion and surveillance that buries its patients under "tons of indifference and oblivion."[10]

Compared to his companions, the writer-narrator, who benefits from his education and social status, is more assured of leaving the hospital. But even he succumbs to hallucinations of enclosure;

> I think they're building a new wall, no, I'm sure of it, and they'll construct other walls that air, space and our dreams can't cross; only our silence will grow, fatten, swell like a mountain.[11]

At a certain point in *Ouarzazate Movie*, a cheerful, unexpected scene provides respite from the ruthless machinery of casting directors and production assistants. In a café, a villager reminisces about time he spent with Pier Paolo Pasolini more than thirty years earlier, in 1966, during the filming of *Oedipus Rex*. He used to carry Pasolini's luggage. They even shared a room. He made good money from the shoot, and bought a little house he is still renovating. It was a shoot unlike any other, and Pasolini was unlike other directors: a highly educated genius, a writer of novels, and a communist.

---

9   Ibid., 134.
10 Ibid., 38.
11 Ibid., 103.

From this short scene, photographer and director Daoud Aoulad-Syad built a feature film titled *Waiting for Pasolini* (2007), set in a small village where most of the older adults worked on *Oedipus Rex* forty years prior. They all remember that shoot as a golden age. It brought pride and income into their lives. Thami in particular, who now repairs TVs and satellite dishes, looks back on it with heartfelt emotion. He assisted Pasolini. He shared his room. In his house, he keeps props from the film set, along with a framed portrait of the maestro. Had he been allowed to spend six months with him, he may have become a great director himself. Instead, he spent four decades pining for an illusion. After drinking by himself late at night, he addresses Pasolini's portrait on the wall: "Who is dead now, you or I?"

Every large film production that comes to town is a godsend. Swarms of children run through the winding streets screaming "the cinema is here! The cinema is here!" This time, an Italian production is announced. A rumour swells that Pasolini is coming back. Everyone turns to Thami. Surely he will be able to secure well-paying jobs for them all through his great communist director friend.

When Thami learns that Pasolini is long dead, he decides to ignore the news, and not tell the other villagers. Meanwhile, just like in *Ouarzazate Movie*, production starts in the absence of a director. Same chain link fence. Same aggravating waits. Same humiliating auditions. Different expectations. Here everyone remains hopeful: when Pasolini shows up, all will be well.

Contrary to Essafi, Aoulad-Syad met Bouanani early on, in the late 80s. He credits Bouanani for instilling in him the desire to make movies when he was still primarily a photographer.[12] This may come as a surprise if one considers that, by then, Bouanani had already given up on directing. Censorship and lack of means made him retreat into writing. He had waited long enough. But as someone who came of age in the immediate wake of Independence, he was acutely aware of the

---

12 Daoud Aoulad-Syad, interview with Roland Carrée in *Répliques* #6, June 2016, 62.

importance and the challenges of building a 'national culture', and remained committed to encouraging young talent. Bouanani mentored Aoulad-Syad's first attempts at filmmaking, editing his first short, *Mémoire ocre* (1991), and writing screenplays for his first feature films, *Adieu forain* (1998) and *Cheval de vent* (2002).

In *Waiting for Pasolini*, Thami is played by a talented actor. Mohammed Majd is apt at conveying the protagonist's peculiar mix of delusion, trepidation, and wisdom. He makes you wonder what might have happened if Pasolini had indeed come back. Or if, back in the day, he had stayed more than a few days or a few weeks. If he had taken an interest in the concrete lives of Moroccan villagers. If, beside sleeping in Thami's room, he had also taught him a thing or two about the craft of images; if he had shown him the kind of selfless generosity Bouanani showed Aoulad-Syad.

Other locations had been considered for *Oedipus Rex*;

> The Romanians had asked me to make a film with them, and I went there to do some location scouting. But I didn't find what I was looking for ... There's no longer anything old in Romania, in the "rustic" sense of the word.[13]

From at least the early 60s, Pasolini considered Europe to be definitively lost to the neo-fascist project of industrialised homogenisation. Africa offered an imagined refuge;

> Ah, the deafening wind / of the desert, the stunning, squalid / sun of Africa that lights up the world. / Africa! My sole / alternative.[14]

---

13 Pier Paolo Pasolini, "Edipo Ré," interview with Jean-André Fiesch, *Cahiers du cinéma* #195, Nov. 1967, p. 14. Authors translation.

14 Pier Paolo Pasolini, 'To Death: A Fragment,' from the collection *The Religion of My Time* (1961), in *The Selected Poetry of Pier Paolo Pasolini*, ed. and trans. Stephen Sartarelli (Chicago: The University of Chicago Press, 2014), 299.

What attracted Pasolini to Morocco was not some specific quality of its people or landscape, but an undefined sense of rustic oldness. The Moroccan south served a simple purpose: it was an ideal surface on which to project his idea of Ancient Greece. Therefore, to imagine that Pasolini might return, or linger, is clearly delusional. He was just passing through. By conceiving of Morocco as an archaic ideal, he failed to see a people waiting, that is, a people desiring transformation.[15]

In *Oedipus Rex*, the population of Thebes, gradually decimated by the plague, awaits a savior. Oedipus is their king, having successfully solved the sphinx's riddle. As despair mounts, the high priest of Thebes, impersonated by Pasolini, makes an impassioned speech begging Oedipus to do something. He is wearing a headdress made of raffia and sea shells. A procession of extras accompanies him—Moroccan faces adorned just like his own, in ostensible solidarity, pleading his plea, hoping his hopes.

This scene has pride of place in *Waiting for Pasolini* where it features three times. The first time, it is a soundtrack to Thami's remembrance of Pasolini in the seclusion of his memorabilia-filled home. The second time, Thami and some friends watch it on the barbershop's tiny TV screen, recognising loved ones among the extras. The third time, they reenact it.

In Ouarzazate, where poverty and abandonment reign supreme, cinema is viewed as a messiah. Everyone's hopes hang on it. Therefore, when the production team abruptly announces the suspension of the film shoot, it feels like a plague has descended upon the village. Even Thami cannot entertain the illusion anymore. He confesses that Pasolini is dead and won't be coming to save the day after all. But he insists that he didn't lie, because his goal was not exactly for his fellow citizens

---

15 Serendipity has it that in 1966, while Pasolini was shooting *Oedipus Rex*, Bouanani too was in the Moroccan desert, a little further west, making his first sort film, *Tarfaya ou la marche d'un poète*. In it a young man walks through the dunes, in search of a legendary poet who might become his mentor—to no avail.

to find work. His goal was "that they believe in something, whatever it is," and he achieved it, since "even those who were fed up with life are now alive again." Armed with that energy, the men of the village accompany Thami on a procession to the film studios, to confront the producers. Thami is wearing the headdress he kept from *Oedipus Rex*. He starts uttering the high priest's speech in broken Italian. By dint of waiting for Pasolini, he has become him.

The high priest performance marked Pasolini's first appearance in one of his fiction films. When asked why he chose to play the priest himself, he said he had found no one in Morocco who was suitable for the role.[16] By forcefully reenacting and adapting Pasolini's speech in front of the production directors, Thami asserts that there is now someone who is.

In *Oedipus Rex*, the speech scene occurs right at the middle point of the movie, when the whimsical historical section gives way to the narration of the myth, to Sophocles' actual words. The priest's speech ushers in tragedy. In *Waiting for Pasolini*, on the other hand, the speech comes at the end. It is not a plea, it is a statement of defiance, an act of collective self-emancipation. The villagers' condition was one of existential waiting marked by the impossibility of being heard; in this scene, they exit silence.

Similarly, there is a chapter in *The Hospital* where the patients embrace a vital experiment in un-waiting. They are feeling even more abandoned than usual. It is raining heavily, and staff has not bothered to come serve them lunch. After some anger and desperation, they decide to get organised and provide for themselves. They cook, they serve, they laugh. For a moment, the courtyard is transformed beyond recognition, the institutional constraints are gone;

---

16 Interview with J.-A. Fieschi, see note 12.

> It was incredible. Not so long ago an atmosphere of despair and degradation had reigned, where I saw nothing around me but sick, motionless men huddled up in the cold, doomed to misery and niggling death; but now I too felt myself come alive.[17]

Toward the end of *The Hospital*, the writer-narrator-patient has a dream in which he is "relentlessly haunted by the idea that the dead don't exist except within us."[18] Before Bouanani died in 2011, Ali Essafi was able to visit with him. Later, he would offer us the gift of Bouanani's voice. His latest documentary, *Crossing the Seventh Gate*,[19] features interviews with the frail, aging mentor alongside excerpts from his movies and various historical documents. By astutely selecting and assembling fragments of a fragile heritage, Essafi reconnects broken lines of transmission; he makes memory speak again. By unearthing and rearticulating marginalised pasts, he opens a path toward possible futures.

In 2001, with *Ouarzazate Movie*, Essafi exposed the imperial ways of the film industry, which captures our landscapes and our labor force while withholding its means of production and projection. In 2006, upon watching Bouanani's short films, he registered a loss, a sustained denial of access to our visual lineage. In 2017, with *Crossing the Seventh Gate*, he recognised that access may never be granted, that we must instead dream our own images out of the memorial rubble. In the process, we might well invent new formats, new narratives, and new political imaginaries.

---

17 Bouanani, *The Hospital*, 83.
18 Ibid., 114.
19 The title makes a reference to *La Septième Porte* [*The Seventh Gate*], a history of cinema in Morocco that Bouanani wrote in the 1980s. The book remained unpublished for over three decades and is only now getting ready to posthumously see the light of day.

Waiting does not empty out time. On the contrary, it occupies the timespace of a slow, radical collective transformation. It fuels a movement of becoming. In Aoulad-Syad's *Waiting for Pasolini*, the villagers were not just waiting, they were getting ready to confront power. Thami was not simply reciting Pasolini's lines night after night in moonlit alleyways, he was rehearsing his becoming-Pasolini, that is to say a figure of creative authority and moral integrity.[20] Ultimately, Thami and the villagers were waiting for themselves. Pasolini was a vessel for their emancipation—a political vessel masked as nostalgia.

"Life ends where it began," says a self-blinded Oedipus at the very end of Pasolini's film. Aoulad-Syad's movie ends as it began—Thami is on someone's roof, fixing a satellite dish. The Italians are gone. Daily life has resumed its course. The main difference with the opening scene is the presence of Thami's young nephew beside him. All of a sudden, festive music is heard. The cinema is coming! The boy is all starry-eyed. But Thami could not care less. He doesn't even turn around. Waiting has ended.

Thami knows now that there is nothing to wait for. The chillingly brilliant ending of Essafi's *Ouarzazate Movie* makes this abundantly clear. We are inside what looks like a high school classroom. A screening event organised by the local film club is about to begin. Someone gives a formal, almost solemn introduction. This is a special program in solidarity with the Palestinian people. He says they would have liked to screen 35mm copies. But Ouarzazate has only two film theatres, and both have been closed for years.

---

20 I borrow the distinction between recitation and rehearsal from Ruth Wilson Gilmore. See for instance her June 2020 podcast conversation with Paul Gilroy, in which she speaks of "the possibility and the intensity of being able to rehearse the future, rehearse the social order coming into being, as against recite the complaints or the demands for that other path, the one that I don't want to take anymore." www.ucl.ac.uk/racism-racialisation/publications/2020/jun/conversation-ruth-wilson-gilmore

After an hour of watching a wealthy industry take advantage of needy villagers, the spectacle of the "rustic" classroom and derelict film theatres is a blow to the heart. Regardless, the special program proceeds. The teenagers watch Palestinian films on a small TV. Who needs a big screen? Solidarity builds from below. There are no white saviours.

The images on the following pages (pp. 168-169) show the 1987 issue of the journal Nejma, with an advertisement reading "Bouanani is seeking a publisher for his book on cinema in Morocco" printed on the back cover. Thirty three years later, a posthumous edition of "La Septième Porte" is finally underway.

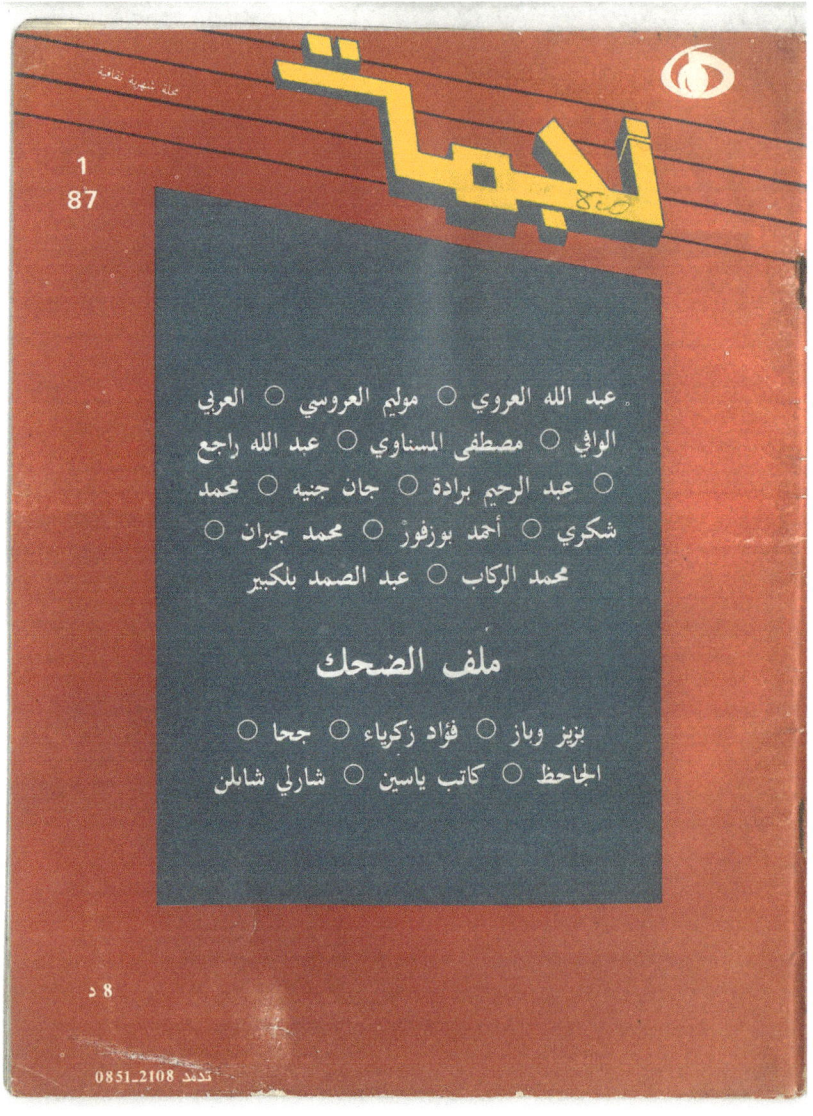

A Tenuous Case of Trust: What to do with a Repeatedly Broken Promise?

Omid Mehrgan

Trust faces the form of a promise. I trust that something said or pledged will be done. Something is put forth (promise) only to be realised in the future. But it is put forward, ultimately if not always, through verbal articulation, in mere words. Both the German verb *versprechen* and the Persian *Ghol-dādán* contain references to speech or saying. In the latter, the speech is given, like in English *giving one's word*. In the former, speaking undergoes a certain modification or distortion: it can be translated as *to misspeak*. The prefix *ver* may also indicate the enforcing of a verb. In any case, it presents an emphatic form of speaking where I put forth my spoken word itself as a deed. Time allies itself with the promiser and the prospect of a future realisation serves as one of the conditions of the trustworthiness of the promise. In short, when I promise something, I say that something will be the case. What does it mean to trust someone's word as a promise? One does not trust the fact that the promised will be the case, but, primarily, the fact that a promise has been made and that promising is possible and valid. External conditions may prevent a promise from being kept and the act from being realised. A broken promise may be forgiven under certain conditions. But the very practice of promising can remain beyond the failure of a particular act of promising. Now, what if the practice itself loses one's trust?

Take the following promise, "I promise that I will not drink again." This is a simple verbal act with no apparent conflict from its presuppositions, at least not yet as we are yet to see if the promise will be kept in the future. This statement deserves trust. It is an act of the practice of promising. The speaker resorts to the practice, relies on the trust of the addressee, and puts forth a resolution that is non-contradictory, possible and probable. It expresses the will to stop drinking and thereby to stop the grave consequences resulting from, say, alcoholism. If the speaker breaks the promise by drinking again, then we have a case of a broken promise. Now suppose the individual says anew: "I promise that I will not drink again." The promise holds, the form of the promise is compatible with the practice of promising, and the content remains plausible. The speaker is trusted with her words and she drinks again. The promise is broken once more. Now if she promises for the third, fourth, fifth time, though all other formal and material conditions of her promise remain the same, something has changed insofar as trusting her promise is concerned—history has been added to the promise as one of its conditions of possibility or, rather, impossibility.

If the one promising has repeatedly broken her promise in the past, like the boy crying wolf in vain after having repeatedly abused that cry, then there is a sense in which this promise is already contradicted by its conditions of possibility—no one believes the speaker. All the same, the promise is no less valid and there is no doubt about the possibility that it can fulfil itself. There is no apodictic reason to say that it will fail this time as it has always failed. However, again, the fact of repeated failures in the past renders the trust in the promise ever more problematic. The formal structure of the promise not to drink ever again and its history of failures come into conflict with each other while both views on the performative hold valid. The result is nothing short of an antinomy. What is most affected by this antinomy is the trust in the act of promising by a single promiser. What is the object of trust in a constantly broken promise? It seems that although the trust in the act of promising may be thereby lost, the trust in the practice of promising as such, that is, the very possibility of human promise, persists.

The case of a repeatedly broken promise introduces a temporal aspect to the promise and the trust, no less. Both acquire a history and a future, a history of failures for the promiser and wounds for the one trusting, and a future of utmost suspicion and fear, if not paranoia. The modality of time in the act of promising and trusting reveals its force more emphatically once we transpose the same structure of a repeatedly broken promise into the spheres of theology, politics, law, psychoanalysis, and aesthetics. Here we will find patterns of antinomian trust that has to deal with each practice and the particular acts of that practice. In each case, recurrent failed promises of divine plan, revolution and elections, reconciliation, and truth and beauty, respectively, introduce a modality of the past into that sphere that works as a condition for trusting the working of that sphere. If each sphere makes up a system of practice with its many individual acts—the practice of theology with particular sermons, or the practice of politics with particular political acts such as constitutions and elections—then trust is to be realised on a double level: trusting the practice as such and trusting the acts of that practice. For instance, I trust that politics creates freedom by making possible a collective form of self-determination in which the people decide their own fate, not monarchs or finance capital or priests or private interests. But, given the repeated failures of a series of otherwise genuine revolutionary movements ending in dictatorship, I hardly trust this or that political act promising a revolutionary break with the previous regime. However, I have to trust this act for it has the formal conditions of political practice, yet, in light of the history of broken words, I tend to regard this act as a repetition of that history. It can very well happen that I might lose faith in the very practice of politics. The burden of the past weighs heavily on the form of the present act.

Three attitudes might follow from this antinomy as ways of resolving the conflict between the practice and the act. First, I adopt an ironic or cynical attitude and regard any act as another failure, as another repetition. Second, I assume a naiveté in virtue of which I continue to believe in the promise of a break with the past put forth by the present political act. In the latter case, there is ample room for corrections, self-criticism, or learning from one's past mistakes, as it were. This naïve trust is premised on a continued firm belief in the practice or the system or the apparatus of politics while classing for modifying its acts. The ironic trust, on the other hand, seems to also give up on the practice, precisely by denying its capacity to generate any trustworthy act. A third attitude is the opposite of the ironic one: here I give up on the practice of politics as such and only believe in radical breaks that particular acts might bring about. Of course, in this case, what is called a 'political' act may have little or nothing to do with the conventional, familiar, tested practice of politics. Imagine that decades of democratic fighting and many elections promising a better society in Iran have come to nothing and the authoritarian rule carries on uninterrupted. I lose all trust in politics and long for a big earthquake or foreign invasion or major terrorist attack as possible ways of toppling the regime. A better example would be the act of the protagonist in Heinrich von Kleist's novella *Michael Kohlhaas*, who, following the failure of a series of legal steps to grant him justice for his two horses taken away from him by a local Junker, loses his faith in the institution of law and takes up arms to restore his rights.

All three solutions to the antinomy of trust faced with a history of failures or broken promises fail to re-establish or revisit the relation between the practice of promising and the particular act of promising. What would be a fourth solution, one that could re-enable trust on a firm ground? In a manner not far from the third, radical solution, but with a minimal, decisive difference, resolving the antinomy involves cancelling out the very distinction between the practice of promising and the act of promising. If the practice—or the institution, the system, the apparatus—with its rules, norms, conventions, and its past, constitute the conditions for the intelligibility and validity of promising acts in various social spheres, then lifting the distinction between the act and its underlying, 'institutional' conditions can have only one outcome: the act has to create its own conditions. This act differs from the third solution in that the latter gives up both on the act and the practice and hope of a total negation of any intelligibility and trustworthiness of the act. A self-conditioned act, on the contrary, avoids complete destruction and refrains from repressing the reality of past failures. It acknowledges the necessity of conditions for the validity of the act. It is not ironic for it believes in the possibility of the act. It is not naïve for it believes in the possibility of the practice backing up the act. In short, the act in the fourth solution is both a case of a practice and not a repetition of an existing one, or: it is a case of a practice yet to come. Of the five spheres mentioned before, theology, politics, law, psychanalysis, and aesthetics, it is only the latter that can offer a model of this self-conditioning act, namely, in art. It is only art that can both remember its past and forget it.

In art, we have on the one hand an apparatus and, on the other, an opus or a particular work of art. That is, the institution of art provides a space in which particular works, no matter how radically different from each other, could be named and known as works *of art*. The *of art* indicates the belonging of statues, painted canvases, compositions of sounds, words, and moving images to a system or institution or practice or apparatus or simply the idea of art with many instances. In this respect, art resembles law, theology, politics, medicine, and other practices. Where it uniquely differs from any other social practice is its claim that it does not have to follow any rules, norms, or conventions associated with the instruction of art. A genuine work of art is not a case of a rule, not an act of a practice, it has no commitment to conform with the general intelligibility of 'artistic practices' and past forms of artmaking. Every work of art claims to be a thing or, rather, an act constituting anew the very meaning of art, and to do so a work of art needs to incorporate all the conditions of artistic practices into its configuration of elements with no need to resort to or rely on something that lies outside of it. A painting may refer to the outside world, to landscapes, people, bridges, posters, but this reference does not constitute its claim to be understood. Every signification, any reference, needs to be anchored in the inner world of the work, entrusted to the specific ways the elements of the work are configured in a complete whole. If you ask a musical piece why this phrase follows that passage, it cannot reliably answer: because that is how previous musical pieces have done it. The reason must be given in the present composition itself. By reconfiguring itself, by incorporating its conditions of possibility or at least by appearing to have done so, the work of art claims to be a radically novel composition of sensuous elements. This claim contains the promise that the work says something about the world that could not be said in any other way or by any other means. The claim goes so far as to say that even when all trust in the institution of art has been lost, this single work *of art* can institute a new practice or open up a new space for doing art.

This will make trust even harder, more fundamentally problematic. For while I normally trust in acts only on account of larger practices within which those acts become recognisable, such as the act of being married to someone within the institution of marriage, in a self-conditioning act there is little evidence beyond the framework of the act itself that could make it intelligible and recognisable and thus trustworthy. But trust is not a passive receptivity. It is not to accept as trustworthy what immediately conforms with common practice. In spite of the wounds it has suffered in its many past disappointments, or perhaps precisely because of those wounds, trust must learn to fight for its promising object, to fight for the possibility of trust again. For, eventually, everything depends on the ability to trust that, to take the ultimate example, collective self-determination through political acts is the only way out of our predicaments. Similar to falling in love, against the backdrop of many historical failures and broken promises, trust in a self-conditioning act actively participates in finding the conditions of the possibility and validity of the act, taking direct part in constituting its object. Just as one immerses oneself with an unprecedented earnestness in a painting to see what it does as if it were the first painting ever created, one falls in love as if for the very first time ever. Although love takes the form of a falling, slipping away, and not of a purposeful, intentional decision, with all the past failures and disillusionments and false promises, with all its well-deserved paranoia casting shadows on any future encounters with others, it must but take up again the trial of trust. For the fate of being together and the possibility of speaking as such depends on one's ability to fall out of one's world of interests, private plans, inclinations, and agendas. In this sense, one *must* fall in love as if for the first time ever, for one must have trust in love or have trust in trust itself.

Contributors

Bani Abidi has been developing a distinctive approach to the moving image for over two decades. She turns to hidden narratives of cities and people, blurring the edges of fictional and actual accounts by accessing the absurd potential of reality. Abidi's videos, drawings and photographic works often stage minor protagonists who shape history as part of everyday living and small acts of resistance within broader dynamics of state power and nationalism. Abidi studied visual art at the National College of Arts in Lahore and at the School of the Art Institute of Chicago. Her solo exhibitions include the Sharjah Art Foundation,(2019); Gropius Bau, Berlin (2019) Neuer Berliner Kunstverein, Berlin (2017); Kunsthaus Hamburg, (2016) among others, and her works are in the collections of several institutions including MoMA, NY; Sharjah Art Foundation, Sharjah; Tate Modern, London and the Guggenheim Museums in New York and Abu Dhabi.

Basma Abdel Aziz is a Cairo-based award-winning writer, sculptor and psychiatrist; specialising in dealing with victims of torture and a long-standing vocal critic of government oppression in Egypt. She is the author of several works of fiction and non-fiction and a columnist in a prominent independent Egyptian newspaper. In 2016 she was named one of Foreign Policy's Global Thinkers for her debut novel *The Queue*, which was also long-listed For the 2017's BTBA and shortlisted for the 2018's TA First Translation Prize. In 2018 She was named by The Gottlieb Duttweiler institute as one of top influencers in the Arab world, and her novel *The Queue* has been translated into Turkish, Portuguese and Italian.

Majd Abdel Hamid splits his time between Ramallah and Beirut. He graduated with a BA in Fine Arts from Malmö Art Academy, Sweden in 2010, and attended the International Academy of Art, Palestine, between 2007 and 2009. He uses a variety of media in his work, including embroidery, video, installation and sculpture, negotiating themes of national identity and trauma. His work has been exhibited at Krognoshuset Lund, Sweden (2016), Valencia Institute of Modern Art, Spain (2018) and Khalil Sakakini Cultural Centre, Palestine (2018). Abdel Hamid has participated in Mediterranea 16, Italy (2013) and the Kathmandu Trienniale, Nepal (2017) as well as Qalandiya International, Palestine (2018). He was a finalist in the A M Qattan Foundation Young Artist of the Year Award in 2008, 2010 and 2012.

Hoda Afshar was born in Tehran, Iran, and is now based in Naarm (Melbourne). Hoda's practice explores the nature and possibilities of documentary image-making. Working across photography and moving-image, she considers the representation of gender, marginality and displacement. Her work has been widely exhibited both locally and internationally. She's represented by Milani Gallery, Brisbane.

Omar Berrada is a writer and curator, and director of Dar al-Ma'mûn library and artists residency in Marrakech. His work focuses on the politics of translation and intergenerational transmission. He has curated exhibitions in Rabat, Marrakech, Rotterdam, Berlin, Dubai, and New York, and edited several volumes, including *The Africans*, a book on migration and racial politics in Morocco (Kulte Editions, Rabat, 2016), and (with Touda Bouanani) Ahmed Bouanani's *La Septième Porte: une histoire du cinéma au Maroc 1907-1986* (Kulte Editions, 2020). His chapbook *Clonal Hum*, a sequence of poems on "invasive species," just came out with Editions Michel Obultra. Other writings in English are included in *The University of California Book of North African Literature* and *Poetic Justice: An Anthology of Contemporary Moroccan Poetry*, among others. Currently living in New York, he teaches at The Cooper Union where he and Leslie Hewitt co-organise the IDS Lecture Series.

Tings Chak is an artist-activist and lead designer and researcher with Tricontinental: Institute for Social Research, a Global South social movement-based institute. Her graphic novel, *Undocumented: The Architecture of Migrant Detention* (2017), explores the role of architecture in the control of migrant bodies and the politics of visual representation.

Hayfaa Chalabi is an illustrator and storyteller interested in the study of governmental restrictions of democratic practices and the role of art to re-contextualise narratives, histories, and discussions. She graduated with a BFA in Visual Communication and Change from Linnaeus University, Kalmar and an MFA in Visual Communication from Konstfack, Stockholm. Chalabi uses her power as an illustrator and storyteller to raise awareness about different socio-political issues. Her work revolves mainly around the misuse of power structures in our society and the intersections of visual culture, gender, and migration.

Sandi Hilal is an architect, artist and educator. currently working on an ongoing art and research project around the concept of hospitality, particularly the Right to be a Host, including the project of the living room. Hilal is the Co-director of DAAR (Decolonizing Architecture Art Residency) co-founded together with Alessandro Petti and Eyal Weizman. Hilal was the head of the Infrastructure and Camp Improvement Program in the West Bank at UNRWA (United Nations Relief and Works Agency for Palestine Refugees in the Near East) from 2008 to 2014. Together with Alessandro Petti, she founded Campus in Camps in 2007

Sepideh Karami is an architect, writer and researcher with a PhD from KTH School of Architecture, Stockholm. Her thesis focused on the idea of Interruption and Dissident architecture developed through writing practices and critical fiction understood as political practices of making architectural spaces. She completed her architecture education at Iran University of Science and Technology (M.A. 2002), and at Chalmers University in Sweden (M.A. 2010). Since 1999, she has been committed to teaching, research and practice in different international contexts and has developed her work through artistic research and interdisciplinary approaches. She has presented, performed and exhibited her work in international conferences and platforms, and is published in peer-reviewed journals. She has been a Lecturer at KTH School of Architecture, since 2018, and is currently a Simpson Postdoctoral Fellow at Edinburgh College of Art, School of Architecture and Landscape Architecture, where she studies (de)colonizing potentials of infrastructure architecture.

Shahram Khosravi is Professor of Social Anthropology at Stockholm University. His research interests include anthropology of Iran and the Middle East, migration, forced displacement, and border studies. Khosravi is the author of the books: Young and Defiant in Tehran, University of Pennsylvania Press (2008); The Illegal Traveller: an auto-ethnography of borders, Palgrave (2010); Precarious Lives: Waiting and Hope in Iran, University of Pennsylvania Press (2017) and After Deportation: Ethnographic Perspectives, Palgrave (2017, edited volume). He has been an active writer in international press and has also written fiction. Khosravi is co-founder of Critical Border Studies, a network for academics, artists, and activists for interdisciplinary studies on borders.

Gunilla Lundahl is a writer and critic in the areas of architecture, design and art. She is co-initiator of the women's collective BIG (Bo i gemenskap) that since the 1970s has been researching co-housing processes. Lundahl has published a variety of books; *Leken och allvaret* (2017) (*Playful and seriousness*) attends to the designers Ulla and John Kandell's practice, *Karaktär och känsla* (2001) (*Character and sensitivity*) discusses a century of Swedish home craft. Lundahl lives and works in Stockholm.

Omid Mehrgan is The James M. Motley Postdoctoral Fellow in the Department of Comparative Thought and Literature at Johns Hopkins University where he received his Ph.D. in Humanities in 2018. His first monograph, *The Narrowest Path: Antinomic of Form in Adorno's Aesthetic Theory Analyzed with Kleist, Hegel, and Marx*, will be published in the Brill Historical Materialism Book Series. In a previous life, he worked as a translator and critic in Tehran, Iran, co-translating works such as Adorno and Horkheimer's *Dialectic of Enlightenment*. His monograph in Farsi entitled *The Theology of Translation: Walter Benjamin and the Task of Translator* was published in 2009. He is based in New York, looking for a job in the pandemic world alongside an army of graduates and academics seeking institutional shelter.

Golrokh Nafisi is an Iranian born visual artist, Illustrator, animator and puppet maker in the contemporary conceptual arts. She graduated from the Rietveld Academie in Amsterdam and studied design at the Art University of Tehran. Nafisi is interested in experimenting with performances in public spaces and discovering new forms of collective action involving bodies and human ideologies.

mirko nikolić is an artist whoes work, both individually and as part of different collaborations and commoning practices, critically examines and prefigures art-making in solidarity with anti-/post-extractivist struggles, healing and regeneration in the wastelands of capitalist-colonial industrial modernity, and commoning/community-making within a multispecies social. This praxis moves transversally between arts and different disciplines of humanities, and shapes into critical writings, place-based performances and cultural organising. Recent and current collaborations evolve through work with Arendse Krabbe, Dori O., Elin Már Øyen Vister, Pluriversal Radio, Sam Skinner. mirko holds a PhD from the University of Westminster, and is currently a postdoc at Department of Culture and Society (IKOS), Linköping University.

Alessandro Petti is an architect who combines research with an architectural, artistic, and pedagogical practice engaged in the struggle for justice and equality. In 2012 with Sandi Hilal he founded *Campus in Camps*, an experimental educational program in the Dheisheh refugee camp in Bethlehem. Petti. together with Sandi Hilal and Eyal Weizman, created DAAR (Decolonizing Architecture Art Residency) in Beit Sahour, Palestine, an architectural studio and residency program that has gathered architects, artists, activists, urbanists, filmmakers, and curators to work collectively on politics and architecture. Petti is co-author of *Architecture After Revolution* (Sternberg, 2013) and *Permanent Temporariness* (Art and Theory, 2019). Petti is Professor of Architecture and Social Justice at the Royal Institute of Art in Stockholm and a Loeb Fellow at Harvard University Graduate School of Design.

Salvatore Porcaro is an architect whose research often combines field work and oral history with the reading of court documents. After completing his research degree in urban planning at the Doctoral School of the IUAV in Venice, he taught Urban Design at the Politecnico di Milano and coordinated projects at the multiplicity lab research laboratory. Recently he founded the Independent Research Agency, an organisation specialising in social research and urban interventions. He has launched a social observatory to study the illegal settlements, the criminal structures and the poverty of the communities living along the northern coastline of Naples in Italy.

Jenny Richards is a curator whose research focuses on questions concerning labour, health and the body, often developed through collaborative practices. She is a PhD candidate at the KTD programme, Konstfack /KTH, Stockholm. Richards was previously co-director of Konsthall C where together with Anna Ahlstrand and Jens Strandberg, developed the exhibition programme Home Works. In 2012 with Sophie Hope, they initiated Manual Labours, a practice-based research project investigating the physical and emotional relationship to work.

Adania Shibli is a Palestinian writer whose novels, plays, short stories and narrative essays have been published in various anthologies, art books, and literary and cultural magazines. She has twice been awarded with the Qattan Young Writer's Award-Palestine; in 2001 for her novel *Masaas* (translated into English as *Touch*. Northampton: Clockroot, 2009), and in 2003 for her novel *Kulluna Ba'id bethat al Miqdar aan el-Hub* (translated into English as *We Are All Equally Far from Love*. Northampton: Clockroot, 2012). Her latest novel is *Tafsil Thanawi* (Minor Detail, Beirut: Al-Adab, 2017). Amongst her non-fiction books are, the art book *Dispositions* (Ramallah: Qattan, 2012), and an edited collection of essays *A Journey of Ideas Across: In Dialog with Edward Said*, (Berlin: HKW, 2014). Along her writing, Shibli is engaged in academic research, and since 2013 she has been teaching part-time at the Department of Philosophy and Cultural studies, Birzeit University, Palestine.

Omid Tofighian is an award-winning lecturer, researcher and community advocate, combining philosophy with interests in citizen media, popular culture, displacement and discrimination. He is Adjunct Lecturer in the School of the Arts and Media, UNSW; Honorary Research Associate for the Department of Philosophy, University of Sydney; member of Border Technologies, University of Oxford; faculty at Iran Academia; and campaign manager for Why Is My Curriculum White? - Australasia. His published works include *Myth and Philosophy in Platonic Dialogues* (Palgrave 2016); he is the translator of Behouz Boochani's multi-award winning book No *Friend but the Mountains: Writing From Manus Prison* (Picador 2018); and co-editor of 'Refugee Filmmaking,' *Alphaville: Journal of Film and Screen Media* (2019).

Faith Wilding is a multidisciplinary artist, writer, and educator. Wilding emigrated to the United States in l961 from Paraguay, where she received her MFA at CalArts where she was a founding member of the Feminist Art Program. Wilding's work addresses aspects of the somatic, psychic, and sociopolitical history of the body. Recent publications, lectures, exhibitions and performances focus on issues of cyberfeminist (women and technology) theory and practice, with particular emphasis on biotechnology. Wilding has exhibited and lectured widely in the USA and Europe. Her audio work has been commissioned and broadcast by RIAS Berlin; WDR Cologne; and National Public Radio, USA. Wilding has published in MEANING, Heresies, Ms. Magazine, The Power of Feminist Art, and other books and magazines. She is the recipient of two individual media grants from the National Endowment for the Arts. Currently, Wilding is a faculty member at the School of the Art Institute of Chicago and the MFA in Visual Art Program at Vermont College of the Union Institute and University.

Cultural Studies

Gabriele Klein
Pina Bausch's Dance Theater
Company, Artistic Practices and Reception

May 2020, 440 p., pb., col. ill.
29,99 € (DE), 978-3-8376-5055-6
E-Book:
PDF: 29,99 € (DE), ISBN 978-3-8394-5055-0

Elisa Ganivet
Border Wall Aesthetics
Artworks in Border Spaces

2019, 250 p., hardcover, ill.
79,99 € (DE), 978-3-8376-4777-8
E-Book:
PDF: 79,99 € (DE), ISBN 978-3-8394-4777-2

Jocelyne Porcher, Jean Estebanez (eds.)
Animal Labor
A New Perspective on Human-Animal Relations

2019, 182 p., hardcover
99,99 € (DE), 978-3-8376-4364-0
E-Book: 99,99 € (DE), ISBN 978-3-8394-4364-4

**All print, e-book and open access versions of the titles in our list
are available in our online shop www.transcript-publishing.com**

Cultural Studies

Andreas Sudmann (ed.)
The Democratization of Artificial Intelligence
Net Politics in the Era of Learning Algorithms

2019, 334 p., pb., col. ill.
49,99 € (DE), 978-3-8376-4719-8
E-Book: available as free open access publication
PDF: ISBN 978-3-8394-4719-2

Jocelyne Porcher, Jean Estebanez (eds.)
Animal Labor
A New Perspective on Human-Animal Relations

2019, 182 p., hardcover
99,99 € (DE), 978-3-8376-4364-0
E-Book:
PDF: 99,99 € (DE), ISBN 978-3-8394-4364-4

Ramón Reichert, Mathias Fuchs,
Pablo Abend, Annika Richterich, Karin Wenz (eds.)
Digital Culture & Society (DCS)
Vol. 4, Issue 1/2018 – Rethinking AI: Neural Networks,
Biometrics and the New Artificial Intelligence

2018, 244 p., pb., ill.
29,99 € (DE), 978-3-8376-4266-7
E-Book:
PDF: 29,99 € (DE), ISBN 978-3-8394-4266-1

**All print, e-book and open access versions of the titles in our list
are available in our online shop www.transcript-publishing.com**